MW00878871

# Grace Not Law!

*The Answer To Antinomianism*

OTHER BOOKS BY THE SAME AUTHOR

UNDER DAVID GAY
*Voyage to Freedom*
*Dutch: Reis naar de vrijheid*
*Christians Grow Old*
*Italian: I credenti invecchiano*
*Battle for the Church (First Edition)*

UNDER DAVID H.J.GAY
*The Gospel Offer is Free (First and Second Editions)*
*Particular Redemption and the Free Offer*
*Infant Baptism Tested*
*Septimus Sears: A Victorian Injustice and Its Aftermath*
*Baptist Sacramentalism: A Warning to Baptists*
*Battle for the Church (Second Edition)*
*The Priesthood of All Believers*
*John Colet: A Preacher to Be Reckoned With*
*The Pastor: Does He Exist?*
*Christ Is All: No Sanctification by the Law*
*Conversion Ruined: The New Perspective and*
*the Conversion of Sinners*
*No Sacerdotalism: A critique of the laying on of hands*
*Eternal Justification: Gospel Preaching to Sinners Marred by*
*Hyper-Calvinism*
*Christians Grow Old (Second Edition)*
*Four 'Antinomians' Tried and Vindicated*

DAVID H.J.GAY: BRACHUS SANCTIFICATION SERIES
*Sanctification in Galatians*
*Sanctification in Romans*
*Sanctification in 2 Corinthians & Philippians*
*Sanctification in Jeremiah*

ALL BOOKS BY DAVID H.J.GAY ARE ALSO ON KINDLE

AUTHOR'S SERMONS CAN BE FOUND UNDER DAVID GAY
at www.sermonaudio.com

# Grace Not Law!

## The Answer To Antinomianism

Paul and Barnabas... urged them to continue in the grace of God
Acts 13:43

## David H.J.Gay

BRACHUS

BRACHUS 2013
davidhjgay@googlemail.com

# Contents

# Introduction

We all know that antinomianism is 'a bad thing'. But what is it? What do antinomians think? What do they do? More important, how can believers be protected against antinomianism?

An antinomian is, literally, one who is *anti nomos* – 'against law', against any law, opposed to the whole notion of law. Within this debate, strictly speaking, an antinomian is a professing believer who will not submit to God's law, one who will not be restrained by it in any form.

But this is where we need to be careful. Consider Paul's words in 1 Corinthians 9:20-21. The apostle speaks of those who were 'under the law', under the law of Moses; namely, the Jews. He speaks of those 'not having the law', those who were destitute of the law of Moses, those who were never given the law of Moses, those who were never under it; namely, the Gentiles. And then he speaks of believers. Referring to himself, Paul explains that though he, as a Jew, had been 'under the law' of Moses, having been converted, he is no longer under that law. Even so, as he says: 'I am not free from God's law but am under Christ's law'. What is more, as the occasion might demand, for the sake of reaching Jews with the gospel, he will re-submit himself to the law of Moses.

In terms of the current debate, none of this is antinomianism. The Jews were under the law of Moses. The Gentiles are not under the law of Moses; God never gave it to them; they are, in this sense, law-less. Believers, while they are not under the law of Moses, are under the law of Christ.

I say all that, reader, to show that the issue is not quite as simple as many Reformed teachers would have us believe. I use it also to encourage you not to be disturbed by those who, with their glib remarks and snide innuendoes, attack those who stand with Paul and declare that believers are not under the law of Moses, but under the law of Christ. Attack in what way? Quite often men smear such believers as 'antinomians'! In so doing, of course, they ought to remember that they slate Paul – along with the rest of us who dare to say the same as he!

Speaking of the Reformed, most Christian teachers, preachers and writers – whether they know it or not – are disciples of John Calvin in this matter: they argue that the way to get believers sanctified, the way to stop them being infected with antinomianism, is to teach and preach the law to them; and by 'the law', they mean the ten commandments, the so-called 'moral law'. Though they have no biblical warrant for any of this, they drive on regardless! Some are overt advocates of this law-system, but many are incipient preachers of rules and regulations in the attempt to produce a people that conform to accepted patterns of behaviour. Those who question, let alone refute, this approach are castigated – and worse – for their pains.

Well, I for one do challenge Calvin's system.[1] I don't do it for the fun of it, of course. Serious consequences are at stake. I am convinced the New Testament sets out a very different way of sanctification. Believers – being in the new covenant – *believers* should not preach the law; *we* should preach Christ! And in our

---

[1] I am not alone, of course! Listen to the following from the 1646 Appendix to the 1644/46 Particular Baptist Confession: 'Though we that believe in Christ are not under the law, but under grace (Rom. 6:14), yet we know that we are not lawless, or left to live without a rule: "not without law to God, but under law to Christ" (1 Cor. 9:21). The gospel of Jesus Christ is a law, or commanding rule unto us; whereby, and in obedience whereunto, we are taught to live soberly, righteously, and godly in this present world (Tit. 2:11-12), the directions of Christ in his evangelical word guiding us unto, and in this sober, righteous, and godly walking (1 Tim. 1:10-11). Though we are not now sent to the law as it was in the hand of Moses, to be commanded thereby, yet Christ in his gospel teaches and commands us to walk in the same way of righteousness and holiness that God by Moses did command the Israelites to walk in, all the commandments of the second table being still delivered unto us by Christ, and all the commandments of the first table also (as touching the life and spirit of them) in this epitome or brief sum: "You shall love the Lord your God with all your heart, *etc.*"' (Matt. 22:37-40; Rom. 13:8-10) (grace-gospel.org). In short: believers are not under the law of Moses, but under the law of Christ.

own experience, we should not be going to the law; we should be going to Christ. 'For the law was given through Moses; grace and truth came through Jesus Christ' (John 1:17). Furthermore, despite the howls of disbelief – and worse – that will greet what I now assert, taking believers to Christ – taking them to grace, not law – far from being the way to antinomianism, is the only way to prevent it!

In my books: *Christ Is All* and *Four 'Antinomians' Tried and Vindicated*, I set out my arguments for these claims. I followed up these volumes with some short addresses on my web page (www.sermonaudio.com/davidhjgay), in which I 'preach' nine of the almost-countless New Testament passages which make the case. As soon as these short talks began to appear on the web, it was clear that they had struck a chord, and my American friend, Ace Staggs – who manages the site for me behind the scenes – asked me if I had the notes of this material. The answer was in the negative: I had spoken extempore. But there was an obvious implication in his question, and I immediately decided to take it up. It wasn't long before Ace had used voice recognition software, and – lo and behold – I could read what I had preached! It is those short discourses which, having been transcribed, make up the contents of this slim volume.

Now for an important caveat: I have published this material with an absolute minimum of editing. While this has obvious – glaringly obvious! – disadvantages, it also has certain benefits. For a start, since the talks are printed almost word-for-word, while this book can stand on its own, it also serves as a script to accompany actual listening to the addresses. Thus the reader can take it in by ear and eye at the same time. Again, by using virtually unedited transcripts of extempore addresses, the material may speak with greater life and power. I hope so.

Of course, although the short discourses were extempore, I have spent a considerable time in these passages when writing my aforementioned books. I didn't say these things off the top of my head! Nevertheless, these addresses were unscripted. Reader, you must bear this in mind. Moreover, if you wish to see my arguments behind what I say, then you should consult my previous works. Above all you should check everything by Scripture.

The new-covenant way of sanctification – the New Testament way of sanctification – is not by the law but by grace. That is my claim. That is what the nine scriptural passages, upon which this volume is based, assert. And that is what I have set out in these pages.

Nevertheless, I do not want merely to make a case. I am convinced the case is irrefutable: sanctification – as justification – is by grace and not law; as is every other aspect of salvation – not least assurance! Very well. In my collected works on this subject, I submit that I have made that case.

In this present volume, however, in addition to demonstrating that is what Scripture teaches, I have a more personal and pastoral concern. I want to do what I can to help the many believers who are in serious trouble over this issue. And there is need! Desperate need! Sadly, too many believers are living a life of bondage and misery through being taken to the law instead of Christ – trying to be sanctified by using the law or imposed rules. They are doomed to failure and disappointment! And many live to prove it! As a result, these believers are often sad, afraid, depressed, spiritually dry, and lacking assurance, as well as finding no help from the law, or those rules, in stimulating them to godliness. Above all, the glory of the person and work of Christ is diminished in their hearts and minds: a grim catalogue indeed!

I hope this slim volume may help believers who find themselves imprisoned in that condition. *And I use the word 'imprisoned' advisedly; see Galatians 3:23; 4:2-3.* By pointing them to Christ, the only one who can relieve and release them, the only one who, by his Spirit, can sanctify them, I hope to help them come into the full liberty of the gospel, and produce a Christ-like life in this pagan world. In short, I desire to see God's people edified, liberated and sanctified, and given back their birthright – a sense, *here and now*, of their ever-increasing glory and inexpressible joy in Christ (2 Cor. 3:17-18; Gal. 5:1; 1 Pet.

1:8-9; for instance). Every believer has – or should have – a triumphant sense of these glorious benefits, NOW! Why? How? Because, in Christ, every believer is perfect in God's sight, every believer is utterly beyond condemnation, every believer is free from all stain, every believer is liberated from law, sin and death, has glory, is being sanctified, and is certain to be taken at last into everlasting bliss, to be like Christ, and to be with him for ever. In Christ, I say, every believer has all this, and has it now, as the Scriptures plainly declare – and declare again and again:

I want you to know that through Jesus the forgiveness of sins is proclaimed to you. Through him everyone who believes is justified from everything you could not be justified from by the law of Moses (Acts 13:38-39).

But now a righteousness from God, apart from law, has been made known, to which the law and the prophets testify. This righteousness from God comes through faith in Jesus Christ to all who believe... A man is justified by faith apart from observing the law... Christ is the end of the law so that there may be righteousness for everyone who believes (Rom. 3:21-22,28; 10:4).

We... know that a man is not justified by observing the law, but by faith in Jesus Christ... We... have put our faith in Christ Jesus that we may be justified by faith in Christ and not by observing the law, because by observing the law no one will be justified... Clearly no one is justified before God by the law, because: 'The righteous will live by faith'. The law is not based on faith; on the contrary: 'The man who does these things will live by them'. Christ redeemed us from the curse of the law by becoming a curse for us, for it is written: 'Cursed is everyone who is hung on a tree'. He redeemed us in order that the blessing given to Abraham might come to the Gentiles through Christ Jesus, so that by faith we might receive the promise of the Spirit (Gal. 2:15-16; 3:11-14).

For just as through the disobedience of the one man the many were made sinners, so also through the obedience of the one man the many will be made righteous (Rom. 5:19).

God made him [Christ] who had no sin to be sin for us, so that in him we might become the righteousness of God (2 Cor. 5:21).

Christ loved the church and gave himself up for her to make her holy, cleansing her by the washing with water through the word, and to present her to himself as a radiant church, without stain or wrinkle or any other blemish, but holy and blameless (Eph. 5:25-27).

Christ came as high priest... He entered heaven itself, now to appear for us in God's presence... He has appeared once for all at the end of the ages to do away with sin by the sacrifice of himself. Just as man is destined to die once, and after that to face judgment, so Christ was sacrificed once to take away the sins of many people; and he will appear a second time, not to bear sin, but to bring salvation to those who are waiting for him... We have been made holy through the sacrifice of the body of Jesus Christ once for all (Heb. 9:11-12,24-28; 10:10).

Therefore, there is now no condemnation for those who are in Christ Jesus, because through Christ Jesus the law of the Spirit of life set me free from the law of sin and death. For what the law was powerless to do in that it was weakened by the flesh, God did by sending his own Son in the likeness of sinful man to be a sin offering. And so he condemned sin in sinful man, in order that the righteous requirements of the law might be fully met in us, who do not live according to the flesh but according to the Spirit (Rom. 8:1-4).

The Lord is the Spirit, and where the Spirit of the Lord is, there is freedom. And we, who with unveiled faces all reflect the Lord's glory, are being transformed into his likeness with ever-increasing glory, which comes from the Lord, who is the Spirit (2 Cor. 3:17-18).

Thanks be to God that, though you used to be slaves to sin, you wholeheartedly obeyed the form of teaching to which you were entrusted. You have been set free from sin and have become slaves to righteousness. I put this in human terms because you are weak in your natural selves. Just as you used to offer the parts of your body in slavery to impurity and to ever-increasing wickedness, so now offer them in slavery to righteousness leading to holiness. When you were slaves to sin, you were free from the control of righteousness. What benefit did you reap at that time from the things you are now ashamed of ? Those things result in death! But now that you have been set free from sin and have become slaves to God, the benefit you reap leads to holiness, and the result is eternal life. For the wages of sin is death, but the gift of God is eternal life in Christ Jesus our Lord (Rom. 6:17-23).

It is for freedom that Christ has set us free. Stand firm, then, and do not let yourselves be burdened again by a yoke of slavery... So I say, live by the Spirit, and you will not gratify the desires of the flesh... If you are led by the Spirit, you are not under law (Gal. 5:1,16-18).

How great is the love the Father has lavished on us, that we should be called children of God! And that is what we are! The reason the world does not know us is that it did not know him. Dear friends, now we are children of God, and what we will be has not yet been made known. But we know that when he appears, we shall be like him, for we shall see him as he is (1 John 3:1-2).

And so on...

*That* is my first aim: I want to instruct, encourage and edify believers, by taking them to the Lord Jesus. I hope, also, that unbelievers might read my book and/or listen to my sermons, and – hearing of Christ in the gospel – be converted. If these ends should be met, it would please me beyond words.

Above all, it would meet my greatest aim – which is to bring glory to the triune God who, in his amazing grace planned this glorious gospel, who, in his unspeakable love accomplished it, and, who, in the fullness of time, by his infinite power, will bring it to complete and everlasting fulfilment in all his elect.

# The Wrong System

# Sanctification: Calvin's System

Though many are completely unaware of it, Calvin's system dominates Reformed and evangelical thinking on sanctification and antinomianism. It is important, therefore, that we should all be clear about Calvin's position on this vital matter. Let me give a sample of the sort of thing Calvin said on the question of the law and sanctification:

The third use of the law (being also the principal use, and more closely connected with its proper end) has respect to believers in whose hearts the Spirit of God already flourishes and reigns. For although the law[1] is written and engraved on their hearts by the finger of God, that is, although they are so influenced and actuated by the Spirit, that they desire to obey God, there are two ways in which they still profit from the law. For it is the best instrument for enabling them daily to learn with greater truth and certainty what that will of the Lord is which they aspire to follow, and to confirm them in this knowledge... Then, because we need not doctrine merely, but exhortation also, the servant of God will derive this further advantage from the law: by frequently meditating upon it, he will be excited to obedience, and confirmed in it, and so drawn away from the slippery paths of sin... The law acts like a whip to the flesh, urging it on as men do to a lazy sluggish ass. Even in the case of a spiritual man, inasmuch as he is still burdened with the weight of the flesh, the law is a constant stimulus, pricking him forward when he would indulge in sloth... It cannot be denied that it [the law] contains a perfect pattern of righteousness... one perpetual and inflexible rule... The doctrine of the law... remains... that... it may fit and prepare us for every good work... The general end contemplated by the whole law [is] that man may form his life on the model of the divine purity... The law... connects man, by holiness of life, with his God.[2]

The law... not only contains a rule of life as to outward duties, but... it also rules their hearts before God and angels.

---

[1] Begging the question as to which law is written on the heart in the new covenant; and getting it wrong – see my *Christ*.
[2] Calvin, John: *Institutes of the Christian Religion*, James Clarke and Co., Limited, London, 1957, Vol.1 pp309-311,356.

The law is the everlasting rule of a good and holy life.
By the word "law"... we understand what peculiarly belonged to
Moses; for the law contains the rule of life... and in it we find
everywhere many remarkable sentences by which we are instructed
as to faith, and as to the fear of God. None of these were abolished
by Christ.[3]

The law... is given for the regulation of the life of men, so that it
may be justly called the rule of living well and righteously... It can
alone direct us to the mark.[4]

[The law] exacts much more of [believers] than they are able to
offer... This is vital... Day by day the law exposes his ungodliness...
The function of the law [is] to sustain [the sense of need], bringing
it home to us continually that all our righteousness is as filthy
rags... It also exasperates and stirs up our depravity... The effect of
the law upon our depraved hearts is akin to the effect of the sun on
any putrid organism. The law suggests sins, even in the very act of
forbidding them. It provokes resentment of God's authority. It
creates a slavish fear of penalty which itself is incompatible with
love, the very essence of obedience.[5]

Martin Bucer said as much before Calvin:

The law... to those who are endowed with the Spirit... is in no sense
abolished, but is so much the more potent in each one as he is
richly endowed with the Spirit of Christ.[6]

And many have followed Calvin:

The moral law does for ever bind all, as well justified persons as
others, to the obedience thereof... The law... is of great use to
[believers]... as a rule of life, informing them of the will of God and
their duty, it directs them and binds them accordingly.[7]

[3] Calvin, John: *Commentaries*, Baker Book House, Grand Rapids,
reprinted 1979, Vol.15 Part 2 p220; Vol.21 Part 1 p119; Vol.22 Part 1
p167.
[4] Calvin, John: 'The Use Of The Law' (sacred-texts.com).
[5] Calvin's Genevan Catechism (quoted by Donald Macleod: 'Luther'
p9).
[6] Wendel, Francois: *Calvin: The Origins and Development of his
Religious Thought*, Collins, London, 1963, p205.
[7] Westminster Confession chapter 19, sections 5 and 6.

The decalogue, or ten commandments... is called the moral law because it is the rule of life and manners... The Scripture is a banquet, and the moral law is the chief dish in it... It is an exact model and platform of religion; it is the standard of truth... Though the moral law is not a Christ to justify us, it is a rule to instruct us... The law of God is a hedge to keep us within the bounds of sobriety and piety... We say not that [the believer] is under the curse of the law, but the commands... The moral law... remains as a perpetual rule to believers... Every Christian is bound to conform to it... Though a Christian is not under the condemning power of the law, yet he is under its commanding power... They who will not have the law to rule over them, shall never have the gospel to save them.[8]

The law was given to be a spur to quicken us to duties. The flesh is sluggish, and the law is... a spur or goad... to quicken us in the ways of obedience.[9]

Although true believers are not under the law as a covenant of works, to be thereby justified or condemned, yet it is of great use to them as well as others, in that as a rule of life, informing them of the will of God and their duty, it directs and binds them to walk accordingly... It... is of use to the regenerate to restrain their corruptions... the law encourages to [their doing good] and deters from [their doing evil].[10]

[The law] is of use to saints and true believers in Christ... to point out the will of God unto them; what is to be done by them, and what to be avoided; to inform them of, and urge them to their duty... to be a rule of life and conversation to them; not a rule to obtain life by, but to live according to... It continues as a rule of walk and conversation to them.[11]

A believer... is under perpetual and indissoluble obligation to conform to [the law] as a rule of conduct... If the [moral] law be not

[8] Watson, Thomas: *The Ten Commandments*, The Banner of Truth Trust, London, 1959, pp10,34.

[9] Bolton, Samuel: *The True Bounds of Christian Freedom*, The Banner of Truth Trust, London, 1964, p83.

[10] The Baptist Confession of 1689, chapter 19.6.

[11] Gill, John: *A Complete Body of Doctrinal and Practical Divinity...*, W.Winterbotham, London, 1796, Vol.2 pp39,41.

a rule of conduct to believers, and a perfect rule too, they are under no rule; or, which is the same thing, [they] are lawless.[12]

A third... and essential use appears to the believer... The believer's sanctification can only be attained in practice by giving him a holy rule of conduct. Such a rule is the law. It is to be assiduously observed as the guide to that holiness which is the fruit of adoption.[13]

The law is a rule of life for believers... [While] the Reformed do full justice to [Calvin's] second use of the law... they devote even more attention to the law in connection with the doctrine of sanctification.[14]

[The law shows] the believer the will of God and his duty to his fellows.[15]

The law of the Lord is not only for the soul that needs conversion, but also for the nurture and warning of the converted.[16]

Avoid as you would a deadly snake any man who denies the law of God is the Christian's rule of life. The law, not the gospel, is the rule of our sanctification.[17]

---

[12] Fuller, Andrew: *Antinomianism Contrasted with the Religion Taught and Exemplified in the Holy Scriptures*, in *The Complete Works of... Andrew Fuller, With a Memoir of his Life*, edited by Andrew Gunton Fuller, Henry G.Bohn, London, 1866, p339; *The Moral Law the Rule of Conduct to Believers in Miscellaneous Tracts, Essays, Letters &c.*, in *The Complete Works of... Andrew Fuller, With a Memoir of his Life*, edited by Andrew Gunton Fuller, Henry G.Bohn, London, 1866, p891.

[13] Dabney, R.L.: *Systematic Theology*, The Banner of Truth Trust, Edinburgh, 1985, p354.

[14] Berkhof, Louis: *Systematic Theology*, The Banner of Truth Trust, London, 1959, p615.

[15] *We Believe: Strict Baptist Affirmation of Faith 1966*, second edition 1973, pp26-27.

[16] Tow, Timothy: *The Law of Moses and of Jesus*, Christian Life Publishers, Singapore, 1986, p29.

[17] A.W.Pink quoted by Murray, Iain H.: *The Life of Arthur W.Pink: His Life and Thought*, The Banner of Truth Trust, Edinburgh, 1981, p104; quoted by Daniel, Curt D.: *Hyper-Calvinism and John Gill*, an unpublished Ph.D. thesis, University of Edinburgh, 1983, p638.

The pedagogic work of the law is not... confined to the unbeliever nor is it confined to our pre-conversion experience. It is vitally important, also, in the life of a Christian.[18]

[Believers] have returned to the moral law for direction in sanctification... Nothing but the moral law can define for us what sanctified behaviour is... As New Testament writers discuss the moral law they frequently and naturally turn to the ten commandments... How is love to God and neighbour to express itself?... To answer this the apostles always return to the ten commandments... How readily the New Testament binds the ten commandments upon Christian consciences.[19]

There it is! This, I submit, is a fair representation of the Reformed system on the law – that system which dominates much of the evangelical world. A grim system, to be sure! And an unbiblical system, to boot!

Reader, before you accept the Reformed way of sanctification, may I suggest you ask for the scriptures which establish the case? Take that last from Chantry: 'The apostles *always* return to the ten commandments... How *readily* the New Testament *binds* the ten commandments upon Christian consciences'. May we be shown this – *from the apostles themselves*?

And, taking my own medicine, that is precisely what ask you to do with me as I now give a few brief expositions of passages from the apostles' writings, plus one from Christ's own great high-priestly prayer for all his people. Making due allowance for the extempore nature of the material, check to see if what I say is a proper exposition of the biblical texts.

And, if you are persuaded that what you read here has got to the heart of New Testament teaching on this vital matter, I urge you to reject man-made systems, and adopt the scriptural way of sanctification and assurance for the believer. It will cost you

---

[18] Macleod, Donald: 'Luther and Calvin on the Place of the Law', The Westminster Conference, 1974: *Living the Christian Life*, p9.

[19] Chantry, Walter J.: *God's Righteous Kingdom: Focussing on the Law's Connection with the Gospel*, The Banner of Truth Trust, Edinburgh, 1980, pp72,84-86,96-97,114.

dear – in terms of rebuke, ostracism and the like – but it will bring you gospel relief and joy. More, it will encourage, stimulate and help you in your daily sanctification and assurance. And it will do this because – instead of directing your mind and heart to the law, to rules, and to looking only at yourself – it will it take you to Christ, it will set your heart and mind on him.

And this is precisely what the apostle commands all believers to do: 'Since, then, you have been raised with Christ, set your hearts on things above, where Christ is seated at the right hand of God. Set your minds on things above, not on earthly things. For you died, and your life is now hidden with Christ in God... Christ is all, and is in all' (Col. 3:1-3,11).

# The Biblical System

Turning from the writings of men, let me take my own medicine – as ladled out at the end of the previous chapter. Let us consult Christ and the apostles. Let us ask them: 'How did you encourage believers to be sanctified? How did you put a stop to antinomianism?'

# Antinomianism: The Antidote

*Dear friends, although I was very eager to write to you about the salvation we share, I felt I had to write and urge you to contend for the faith that was once for all entrusted to the saints. For certain men whose condemnation was written about long ago have secretly slipped in among you. They are godless men, who change the grace of our God into a license for immorality and deny Jesus Christ our only Sovereign and Lord... These are the men who divide you, who follow mere natural instincts and do not have the Spirit. But you, dear friends, build yourselves up in your most holy faith and pray in the Holy Spirit. Keep yourselves in God's love as you wait for the mercy of our Lord Jesus Christ to bring you to eternal life. Be merciful to those who doubt; snatch others from the fire and save them; to others show mercy, mixed with fear – hating even the clothing stained by corrupted flesh. To him who is able to keep you from falling and to present you before his glorious presence without fault and with great joy – to the only God our Saviour be glory, majesty, power and authority, through Jesus Christ our Lord, before all ages, now and forevermore! Amen (Jude 3-4,19-25).*

I want to speak to you for a few minutes on the book of Jude.

Jude told his readers that he had wanted to write to them about the salvation we share, but, as he came to write, he saw that there was an even more pressing issue about which he should write. Verse 3: he felt that he should write to these believers and urge them to contend for the faith that had been entrusted to all the saints once and for all. The reason, as he says in verse 4, is that certain men – false teachers – had infiltrated the churches, come among the believers. And what they were doing was taking the gospel, the grace of God in the gospel, and they were changing, warping, twisting, distorting that grace of our God into a licence for immorality, and ultimately denying the Lord Jesus Christ, our only sovereign and Lord. They were taking the liberty which believers have in Christ, under the gospel, in the new covenant – the liberty, the freedom from sin, from death, and from law – and they were warping this freedom – distorting it, twisting it into licence for immorality.

The long word for this is 'antinomianism' – *anti*: against; *nomos*: law – lawlessness, if you will; utter lawlessness; do as you want; live as carnally as you please. Another word for it is [libertinism] – a person who teaches like this is 'a libertine'. A person who practices this is 'a libertine': antinomianism, libertinism.

These people take the grace of God, and push it to such an extent, and warp it in such a way, as they teach believers that they can sin as much as they like, they can be as carnal as their flesh desires, and they do not in any way bring upon themselves any consequences! In fact, some will go so far as to say that they would magnify the grace of God the more they sinned.

This, of course, is an appalling doctrine. The practice is utterly evil.

Believers *have* to be holy: 'Holiness without which no man shall see the Lord'. And that does not speak about justification, there! That speaks about sanctification! Godliness! Christ-likeness! Unless a man is a new creature, and lives as a new creature, he has not passed from death unto life! He is still in the kingdom of darkness!

And Jude sees this problem, this issue, in the churches, and he feels he must write and contend for the gospel – the gospel that has been once been given to the saints, entrusted to us by God in his grace.

From verse 5 to verse 19, Jude expands on this, and gives illustrations and examples of it: the Israelites sinning coming out from Egypt, the angels who fell, Sodom and Gomorrah, and so on; Balaam, Korah. And Jude is very clear how evil and corrupting and warping and corroding – corrosive – is this doctrine.

Now, the issue is – he wants to put it right: How can we stop believers sinning? How can we promote godliness amongst believers? What is the motive for it? How will we be spurred, as believers, to live lives that glorify God in Christ?

Well, historically – it didn't begin with Calvin – but Calvin formulated it more clearly than any – Calvin said that we do this – we promote godliness, we produce sanctification – by the law of Moses, by the law of God, particularly the ten commandments. He described the law as a whip. He described believers as lazy asses, or lazy donkeys or mules. And to make us holy, as lazy asses, as he called us, we need to be whipped with the law.

Calvin's view has dominated the Reformed and evangelical world ever since. And even to this very day, the vast majority of Reformed and evangelical people are convinced that sanctification is by the law: it gives us the standard of sanctification, and it moves us and motivates us, and spurs us to it. Some evangelicals and Reformed are overtly, and definitely, clearly, Calvinistic in this way. But perhaps the majority of evangelicals are unknowingly following Calvin in this way, and, although they, perhaps, wouldn't be as overt as saying the law is the great sanctifier – the great spur and motive for our sanctification – nevertheless they fall into what I can only call 'recipe preaching': do this, do the other, stop doing that, tick the boxes – and, lo and behold, you will be sanctified! Conform to certain rules (often man-made), and you will be sanctified! 'Recipe preaching'! 'List preaching'! And, underneath it all, fear is the motive. The whip makes the lazy donkey cower. The burnt child fears the fire. The lazy ass cowers at the whip. And, for the majority of Reformed and evangelical believers, fundamentally – at the bottom – *fear* is the motive for sanctification.

Let us get back to Jude.

Up to up verse 19, he's been explaining the problem, but, from verse 20 to the end of his book (to verse 25), he gives the solution to antinomianism, the antidote. He starts: '*But* you, dear friends'; '*but* you, dear friends...' You see: he changes gear at verse 20.

All I want to do in these few minutes is ask you just to look at the book of Jude, and see for yourself. How does Jude motivate me as a believer? How does he motivate you as a believer to live a godly life for Jesus? How does he protect these believers from these false teachers, these antinomians, these libertines?

Well... it's quite clear to me! Look at verses 20 to 25. Examine these verses for yourself. If you ask Calvin, if you ask the Reformed, if you ask the evangelicals, the majority, fundamentally their answer is this: 'The law! Preach the law to them! Hammer the law! Take them to the law! *That* will prevent them from following the antinomians!'

Now look at Jude. Read verses 20 to 25.

How many times does Jude say 'the law', 'the law'? Well... I cannot see that he uses the words 'the law' once! What he does say, the words he does use are these, words like: 'The Holy Spirit... God's love... the mercy of our Lord Jesus Christ... being merciful... show mercy'. *These* are the kinds of words that I see Jude using here. He's not taking them to the law, is he? Where *is* he taking them? He's taking them to grace, not law! He's taking them to the gospel, not to the law. He is taking them, above all, to the Lord Jesus Christ, and not the law.

You see, the answer to antinomianism is *not* the law. The way to produce holiness is *not* to preach the law. It is to preach *Christ*. It is to look to Christ, to consider Christ, to meditate upon Christ, to grow up into Christ, to want Christ, to want to please Christ.

Now this is only one passage, and I haven't time to give all the arguments. I can only suggest that you look through the New Testament. Say, take Romans 12 to the end, and count how many times the apostle talks about 'the law'. He does, in those verses, use the law as a paradigm or an illustration – in one passage – but see how many times in that great passage, where he is speaking about sanctification (Romans 12 to the end) – how many times does he say: 'Christ', 'Christ', 'Christ'? If you wish to see my full arguments, may I suggest you read my books: *Christ Is All* and *Four 'Antinomians' Tried and Vindicated*? But, above all, read the New Testament, and see, mark, how, whenever Paul or Peter or John, or any of the apostles, urge upon us sanctification, the motive they use, the spur that they use, is always Christ and the grace of God in Christ. This stands out a mile!

Let me give you one or two examples. Paul tells the Corinthians – tells us – that we should cleanse ourselves from all filthiness of the flesh. I'm thinking of 2 Corinthians 7, verses 1 and 2. The passage leads on from chapter 6. Now what is the motive for cleansing ourselves? Is it the law? Well, read it and see! He speaks of the wonderful promises that God has given us in the gospel in Christ. This is the way to be sanctified: through the Lord Jesus Christ!

Take another place: Ephesians 5. We have to forgive other believers. Why should we forgive others? 'Even as God for Christ's sake has forgiven us'.

I already mentioned Romans 12 to 16. But it's right throughout the New Testament: the motive, the spur for sanctification is always Christ and the gospel, the grace of God. It is never the law.

I say to you my friends, in Jude's words: 'But you, dear friends, build yourselves in your most holy faith, and pray in the Holy Spirit'! You need to be protected from antinomians. You need to be stirred to godliness and holiness and spiritual life, if you are a believer. And this is how you do it:

Dear friends, build yourselves up in your most holy faith and pray in the Holy Spirit. Keep yourselves in God's love as you wait for the mercy of our Lord Jesus Christ to bring you to eternal life. Be merciful to those who doubt; snatch others from the fire and save them; to others show mercy, mixed with fear – hating even the clothing stained by corrupted flesh.

If you look to the Lord Jesus Christ, if your business is to see others looking to the Lord Jesus Christ, and rescue them from their sins, the antinomians will not gain ground on you. The answer, the antidote, to antinomianism is not the law. The great motive is Christ and the gospel. And, I say, if you continue – and if I with you – if we all continue to grow in the grace and in the knowledge of our Lord and Saviour Jesus Christ, we shall experience what Jude speaks of in his final verses, this great doxology:

To him who is able to keep you from falling and to present you before his glorious presence without fault and with great joy – to the only God our Saviour be glory, majesty, [and] power and authority, through Jesus Christ our Lord, before all ages, now and forevermore! Amen.

Believer! How were you washed from your sins? How were you justified, and brought to peace with God? It was through our Lord Jesus Christ, was it not? You looked to him. You knew that if you believed on the Lord Jesus Christ, you would be saved. And so you looked, you believed, and you were saved. How will you be sanctified? Continue to look to the Lord Jesus Christ. Grow up into him in all things. Consider him! Set your heart, your mind, your affections on Christ. Christ is all!

Unbeliever – if there's an unbeliever listening to me – you need to be saved. You are a sinner; you're on the road to damnation. The only way to be washed from your sins and put right with God is looking by faith, coming by repentant faith, turning to the Lord Jesus Christ, and believing on him, trusting him. Do so, now!

And believer! Look to Christ! Continue to look to Christ! And you will grow in grace. And you will come to that place where you will have everlasting glory, and be with Jesus for ever more! And until that time, you will continue to experience his work of sanctification by his Spirit within you.

# Antinomianism: Its Preventative

*If we walk in the light, as he is in the light, we have fellowship with one another, and the blood of Jesus, his Son, purifies us from all sin. If we claim to be without sin, we deceive ourselves and the truth is not in us. If we confess our sins, he is faithful and just and will forgive us our sins and purify us from all unrighteousness. If we claim we have not sinned, we make him out to be a liar and his word has no place in our lives. My dear children, I write this to you so that you will not sin. But if anybody does sin, we have one who speaks to the Father in our defence – Jesus Christ, the righteous one. He is the atoning sacrifice for our sins, and not only for ours but also for the sins of the whole world. We know that we have come to know him if we obey his commands. The man who says: 'I know him', but does not do what he commands is a liar, and the truth is not in him. But if anyone obeys his word, God's love is truly made complete in him. This is how we know we are in him: Whoever claims to live in him must walk as Jesus did (1 John 1:7 – 2:6).*

I would like a few words with you on 1 John and chapter 2 and verse 1; the first letter of John, the second chapter, and the first verse. John, writing to believers, says this: 'I write this to you so that you will not sin'. 'I write this to you so that you will not sin'. As I say, he is writing to believers – those who have a living faith in our Lord Jesus Christ – and he is writing, he is concerned, that he should prevent them from sinning; he should do what he can to raise up a barrier against them sinning. In other words, he wants them to be holy; he wants them to be godly; he wants them to grow in grace and in the knowledge of our Lord and Saviour Jesus Christ; he wants them to be a spiritual people. Again, in other words, he's raising a barrier against antinomianism; he's raising a barrier against licentiousness, carnality, worldliness. He wants these believers to be as spiritual as they can be. Murray M'Cheyne, I believe, used to pray: 'God make me as holy as a man can be'. 'My dear children, I write this to you so that you will not sin'.

Now this is a very important matter. It's a current debate. If you ask the majority of believers, teachers, the answer they will give will be along the lines of: the way you prevent believers from sinning is by teaching them the law, and reminding them, reminding them very strongly, that now that they are justified by faith, they are now under the law of God, the law of Moses – the ten commandments in particular, 'the moral law', as they call it – they are under that law for sanctification. This was not started by John Calvin – but he certainly formulated it! But the majority of evangelicals are in this system. They believe that by teaching the law they will make men, believers, holy. It won't save them. They know that: it won't justify them. But they know that once a man – or they believe, that once a man is justified, they argue, he is under the law for sanctification.

The interesting thing is, let's ask the apostle; let's ask John. After all, this is his expressed and stated aim: 'My dear children I write this to you so that you will not sin'. He's on the same page – he, and these other teachers I'm talking about, have the same end and purpose and goal: they want to prevent believers from sinning and they want to make believers as holy as possible. Many modern teachers say: 'The law!' Now, what does say John say? 'These things, I write this...'. '*These* things I write to you so that you will not sin'. Now... what things?

Well let's just go a little before, and a little after. I think that's fair. What did he say just before? Well, I read things like this:

The blood of Jesus, God's Son, purifies us from all sin... If we confess our sins, God is faithful and just and will forgive us our sins and purify us from all unrighteousness.

And if I go just a little after, I see this:

We have one who speaks to the Father in our defence – Jesus Christ, the righteous one. He is the atoning sacrifice [the propitiation], for our sins, and not for ours only but also for the sins of the whole world.

I put it to you that when John says: 'My dear children, I write this, I write these things to you', the things he's talking about are the blood of Christ, the forgiveness of sins through the righteousness and the blood of Jesus Christ, his propitiation, his sacrificial death to atone for the sins of his people, and to take the wrath of God for them: that *these* are the things that John writes.

He's not writing, he says, this so that unbelievers will be converted. I mean... certainly these doctrines would be very helpful to put before unbelievers that they might be saved, and converted, and brought to faith, and justification, the blood of Christ, the forgiveness of sins. But he is not writing to unbelievers here. He's writing to believers: 'My dear children... walking in the light'. He's talking *about* believers, and he's talking *to* believers. And yet the very things that he stresses here – he says that these very things – are the ones 'I write so that you will not sin'.

Now is this not staggering? in the light of the contemporary church I mean, the contemporary teachers. 'The law, the law, the law'! What does John stress? 'The blood of Christ, the righteousness of Christ, the sacrifice of Christ, Christ's propitiation'. 'I write *these* things. I *stress* these things. I *preach* these things', he said. 'I *teach* these things to believers'. Why? Because it is *these* things above all: Jesus Christ, *Jesus Christ* preached, the *blood* of Christ preached, the *forgiveness* of sin preached. *That* is the way to sanctify saints.

If anybody quarrels with that, read the full argument in chapter 2 verse 1. 'My dear children, I write this to you so that you will not sin. But if anybody does sin we have...', and then he goes on to speak of the Lord Jesus Christ. In other words, this *is* the very doctrine that he puts before us. 'Believer', he said, 'think about the Lord Jesus Christ. Think about his death for you. Think about his blood washing away your sins. Think about the love of God towards you, in giving – not sparing – his Son, but delivering him up for you. Think about the fact that he took the wrath of God for you. Meditate upon Christ. Set your heart upon Christ. And you will grow like him. Look to him, and you will become like him'. And being like Christ is being holy. *This* is what holiness is: Christ likeness.

If you have to plough a furrow in a field, and you want to plough a straight furrow, the secret is this: go to one side of the

33

field, the far distant side, and plant a stake there, raise a stake there. Come back to the other side of the field, and start to plough. And keep your eye fixed on that stake! You won't make a perfect line, but if you look down on the ground, or you look around you, you will go all over the place! Fix your eyes upon the stake, and you will plough a straighter furrow. Fix your eyes upon Jesus! Consider him! Set your eyes upon him! '*These* things I write to you that you will not sin'.

And it goes even deeper and more wonderful than that!

John says: 'I don't want you to sin, and I'm writing this so that you won't sin. But if you do sin, if you do fall, the blood of Christ still washes you from your sins! He, in his righteousness, presents you perfect, faultless, before the Father, without condemnation!'

I think we have to be honest here. This sounds mad, doesn't it! To tell believers not to sin – but then to tell them that, if they do sin, Christ's blood will take it all away! Surely this will not stop sin! Surely this will be antinomianism! Surely this will not produce holiness! You must preach the law!

And I'm sure that will be the reaction of some who will be listening to me.

Your quarrel, my friend, is not with me. I've not said it. Well... I have, but I am the messenger boy here. I've got a Bible open in front of me, and I'm just declaring to you what John says. Your quarrel is not with me – it is with John, the apostle! Ultimately, your quarrel is with God, the Holy Spirit! For *he* wrote through John!

Now I know your creeds and your Confessions and your theological books will tell you it is the law, the law, the law that will sanctify. But I'm telling you what John said. He says: 'It's thinking about Jesus. Stress these things – I stress these things; I write these things'. When Paul wrote to Titus – you will find it in chapters 2 and 3 – he says it the same thing. He tells Titus to 'stress *these* things – these very same things – to make the saints holy. In fact, it says it throughout the New Testament! The way to stop antinomianism? The way to produce holiness? Law? It is Christ!

'Ah!' you say: 'But go on to verse 3: "We know that we have come to know him if we obey his commands; and so on". There you are! You have the law. "The law" there's the ten commandments. There's the moral law'.

There's two things I want to say about that. John has said these things about Christ and his sacrifice all clustered around my text. True, in the slightly wider context, we do have the word 'commands', 'commands', and so on. Yes! But the first thing I want you to see is this: in the immediate context, the things that are stressed are the blood and sacrifice and righteousness of Christ! There's no gainsaying it! 'The commands' are there, but they come *after* this great truth I have put before you. That's the first thing I want to say.

But there's another thing, too! You're making a very, very big assumption here: 'commands', 'ten commandments', 'moral law'. Oh? Where did you get that? It says, in my Bible: 'We know that we have come to know him if we obey his commands'. 'Him', 'his'! These are what we call pronouns. The pronoun is in the place of a noun, and it refers back to the noun that comes immediately before. And let's go back and see who the 'him' and 'his' are. Ah! I've got it! '*He* is the propitiation', in verse 2. Ah! Who is the 'he'? Lets go back to verse 1: 'Jesus Christ the righteous one'. Now verse 3: '*His* commands are...' *Jesus Christ's commands!* 'If a man loves *me* he keeps *my* commands'.

I'm not saying a word against the ten commandments, but I'm telling you that the law that's in question in verse 3 is the law of *Christ*, the commands of *Christ*. It doesn't give any weight at all to those theologians and doctors and teachers and preachers and writers who tell us that we have to come under the moral law, as they call it, the ten commandments, the law of Moses, for sanctification. The whole context here is Christ, Christ, Christ: his death and his law. It's the old text, Colossians 3:11, again and again: 'Christ is all'!

Believer, would you be sanctified? Then look to Christ! Gaze upon him! Think about his love for you, his death for you, his blood shed for you! that you are perfect, free from condemnation in the sight of God! And let this melt your heart, and move your soul, and govern your life, so that you yield obedience, loving Christ, and keeping his law.

If there is an unbeliever listening to me: this doctrine is for believers; this teaching is for believers. But there's an application to you! Would you be saved from your sins? And you desperately need salvation, I tell you! There is only one way. If John says to believers: 'My dear children, I write this to you so that you will not sin... Christ, Christ, Christ', I am more than justified in saying to you: 'Unbelieving friend... if you would be saved: Christ, Christ, Christ, Jesus, Saviour. Take him as your Saviour, Christ, Messiah, the anointed one. Take him as your Messiah, Lord. Take him as your King. Submit to him – the Lord Jesus Christ. Look to him, and you will be saved!'

So, whether you're a believer, or an unbeliever, this text is saying the same thing: 'Behold the Lamb of God!' He takes away sin. He sanctifies the saint. Look to him! Be saved, and sanctified.

# Antinomianism: What To Stress

*At one time we too were foolish, disobedient, deceived and enslaved by all kinds of passions and pleasures. We lived in malice and envy, being hated and hating one another. But when the kindness and love of God our Saviour appeared, he saved us, not because of righteous things we had done, but because of his mercy. He saved us through the washing of rebirth and renewal by the Holy Spirit, whom he poured out on us generously through Jesus Christ our Saviour, so that, having been justified by his grace, we might become heirs having the hope of eternal life. This is a trustworthy saying. And I want you to stress these things, so that those who have trusted in God may be careful to devote themselves to doing what is good. These things are excellent and profitable for everyone. But avoid foolish controversies and genealogies and arguments and quarrels about the law, because these are unprofitable and useless (Tit. 3:3-9).*

I would like to speak for a few minutes on Titus chapter 3 and verse 8; Titus chapter 3 and verse 8. It's these words that I'm interested in at this time: Paul, writing to Titus, says this: 'I want you to stress these things, so that those who have trusted in God may be careful to devote themselves to doing what is good. These things are excellent and profitable for everyone'. 'I want you to stress *these* things, so that those who have trusted in God may be careful to devote themselves to doing what is good'.

Well, I don't think there's any difficulty in understanding what the apostle means here! We can see, very clearly, the people he has in mind. It stands out, very clearly: those who have *trusted* in God; in short, believers. That is: not those who have just accepted the facts about the existence of God, but who know God as their Father because the Lord Jesus Christ is their Saviour. They have trusted him. They have turned from their sins in repentance. They have called upon the name of the Lord, and they are saved. They are justified. They are right with God. They are washed in the blood of Jesus Christ. They are clothed with the perfection of his righteousness. They have peace with God: justified.

Paul is concerned about these believers, and what happens *after* their conversion. By coming into Christ, by faith, [having been] born again of God's Spirit, and then believing and repenting and turning to God through the Lord Jesus Christ, the Spirit has come into them, and they are new creatures in Christ Jesus.

If I'm speaking to a believer – here, now – as I say these words: 'You, my friend, this is what has happened you. You have been born again of God's Spirit. You have brought to trust in Christ. And it's said of you, as Paul writes to Titus: "I want you to stress *these* things, so that those who have trusted in God..."; and so on'. So I am addressing believers here – as Paul was addressing Titus about believers here. There's no problem with that.

Nor is there any problem, any question, any doubt, about what he wants. He wants these believers to 'be careful to devote themselves to doing what is good'. And the rest of his letter, and the rest of the New Testament, tells us what that is: the good works that follow out of our being justified. The good works do not contribute to our justification, but they are the outworking of our justification! But this is called 'sanctification', being made godly, being made obedient to Scripture, being conformed more and more to our Lord Jesus Christ. 'As I, so you', is the essence of New Testament sanctification. The standard before us, the merits of the person and work of the Lord Jesus Christ, his accomplishments – there's the perfection – and as we are transformed into his image – this is what Paul was talking about here: 'be careful to devote themselves to doing what is good'. Not to earn, not to merit their salvation. But because they are saved, they will want to do it; because they are saved, they must do it. God has created us anew in Christ that we might live for his glory.

Now, I say, I don't think there's any problem about any of the things I've said so far.

But here we run into the buffers! Or, if I change the picture, here we come to the crossroads, or the fork, rather – the fork, yes, that's better – we come to a fork in the road! The *great* question is, the penetrating question is: How shall we attain to this standard? What method does Paul press upon Titus to bring these believers to this godliness and spirituality of walk and life?

Now, it is a fact – whether evangelicals and Reformed people realise it – it is a fact that the majority of the evangelical world believes that the way to reach this standard of holiness, and to reach this growth in experience and knowledge of Christ, and likeness to Christ, the way to reach that is for the preachers to preach to us the law, the ten commandments – as they call it 'the moral law'. By pressing upon us the law, by our meditating upon the law, seeing the standard of the law – bearing in mind that, if we sin, there is punishment, so there's an element of fear in it; there's more than an element, for John Calvin, who formulated this system, which has so dominated the evangelical world, said that the law was like a whip hitting lazy asses, lazy donkeys. And this system, Calvin's system, has dominated the evangelical and Reformed world for these past hundreds of years. And, even on a lower level, incipient level, a hidden level, as it were, much contemporary preaching and view of sanctification is: Conform to the rules! Meet the standards set upon you, especially by the teachers of the churches, and so on, then this will bring sanctification! The creeds, the Confessions, the systematic theology's, the writers, the preachers – they nearly all say this: it's the law!

I ask you! Paul tells us here! What does he say to Titus? He says: 'I want you to stress *these* things, so that – in order that, with this purpose – that those who have trusted in God might be careful – thoughtful – to devote themselves to good works – to what is good. *Stress **these** things!*'

Well, Paul, what things did you want him to stress? Well, he would say to me: 'Read what I said! Take it up at verse 3. You will see what we were: "Foolish, disobedient, deceived, enslaved by all kinds of passions and pleasures". Right! "We lived in malice and envy"; and so on. Now, then, come to verse 4: "But when the kindness and love of God our Saviour appeared, he saved us". Notice it goes on: "Mercy... saved us...

rebirth... renewal by the Holy Spirit... poured out on us generously through Jesus Christ our Saviour... justified by his grace... heirs having the hope of eternal life. This is a trustworthy saying". And I want to stress *these* things, so that those who are trusting, have "trusted in God, may be careful to devote themselves to doing what is good" – good works, good things'.

Stress *what*? The mercy of God, the love of God in Christ, the regenerating power of the Spirit: the gospel, in other words, the righteousness of our Lord Jesus Christ, the generosity of God through Jesus Christ our Saviour, our justification. 'Preach this', Paul says to Titus: '*Stress* this in your conversations, in your preaching ministry, in anything you say or do or think. *Stress* this!'

I ask: 'Where is the law, here?'

Well!... I'm waiting... Where is the law, here? What is Paul's motive for sanctification? What does Paul stress? He uses that very word: 'stress'! What does he want Titus to stress? What does he want me to stress to you, now?

Believer, would you be holy? Then look to Christ! Remember what God has done for you in Christ: for he has saved you from your sins, and washed you, transformed you, brought you into the kingdom of light – out of the kingdom of darkness. Think of his mercy to you. Think of Christ!

Stress *these* things!

Believer! Look to Christ – not to the law! Any preacher hearing me, any writer hearing me, any theologian hearing me: Give up this stressing the law! Preach Christ, my brother and sister. Preach Christ! Look to Christ, my brother and sister. Rest upon Christ, the mercy, the love, the kindness of God in Christ, the power of the Spirit: 'The law of the Spirit of life in Christ Jesus has set me free from the law of sin and death'!

And as I concentrate more and more upon Christ, and the gospel, increasingly shall I find myself drawn to him, and so produce fruits in my life to the glory of God.

And if I sin, I'm sinning against *this* love, and *this* mercy, and *this* forgiveness, *this* God – it's not against the law. It's not fear: it's *love*! Love casts out fear, but where there is fear there is no love. Cast out the fear, my brother and sister! Let us look to Jesus, let us look to him alone.

Notice how the apostle goes on: 'But avoid foolish controversies and genealogies and arguments and quarrels about the law, because these are unprofitable and useless'.

If Paul was standing here now, and I said to him: 'Paul should I preach law or gospel?' – what would his answer be? 'Should I get embroiled in the law, or should I get to lifting up Christ?' 'What should I do, Paul?' I think his answer is unmistakeable: '*Preach Christ* to them – until Christ is formed in them!'

And I say that to myself – even as I preach him now, as I write about him: 'Oh! that my soul could *love **him*** more – the Lord Jesus – more and more, be conformed to him!'

If there is an unbeliever listening to me, these words have been said to believers. As Paul wrote to Titus, it was for those who have trusted in God. Now you have not trusted in God. You're an unbeliever! Well that which will sanctify us is that which saved us in the beginning. And it will save you, my friend! It's not 'it' at all! It is the Lord Jesus Christ! You are a sinner, and you will come under – well, you are under the wrath of God now – and you will suffer it for ever, if you die in your sins. But, as this passage says, from verse 3 on, if you look to Christ, if you trust in the mercy and kindness of God, if you call upon the name of the Lord, you will be saved, and everlastingly freed from your sins. Then you, too, will begin, with us, this pilgrimage of looking more and more unto Jesus, more and more reflecting, meditating upon, and rejoicing in, and singing about, and talking about, and thinking about, the great mercy of God toward us in our Lord Jesus Christ. And this will glorify God – in the saving of sinners and the sanctifying of saints!

41

So... sinner look to Christ, now! Saint! Go on looking, looking to Jesus!

# Sanctification Not By The Law

*Sanctify them by the truth; your word is truth. As you sent me into the world, I have sent them into the world. For them I sanctify myself, that they too may be truly sanctified. My prayer is not for them alone. I pray also for those who will believe in me through their message (John 17:17-20).*

I would like to speak to you for a few minutes on John chapter 17, and verse 17; John chapter 17, and verse 17. Jesus, in his great prayer in the garden, says: 'Sanctify them by the truth; your word is truth'. 'Sanctify them by the truth; your word is truth'.

He is praying here for his people. At the moment, he's praying for his immediate disciples. But as he goes on – in verse 20 – to say: 'My prayer is not for them alone. I pray also for those who will believe in me through their message' – through the apostolic preaching. We may, therefore, justly, regard this prayer of Christ: 'Sanctify them by your truth; your word is truth', we may justly take this to be a prayer for us – if we are believers. A prayer for us today!

So, I address you as a believer. If you are a believer in our Lord Jesus Christ, one of whom it says, in the beginning of this chapter, that you have come to know the only true God through Jesus Christ, you have trusted him, you have rested your soul and your eternity upon him, for your everlasting salvation, his blood has washed you from your sins, if his righteousness has clothed you, Jesus is praying for you here – in this great prayer: 'Sanctify them'! 'Sanctify these believers, sanctify all believers, by the truth'! And as he says to his Father: 'Your word is truth'!

Now, I want to speak to you, at this time, on this matter of sanctification; on this matter of avoiding antinomianism, overcoming antinomianism. Antinomianism and sanctification[1] are exact opposites: godliness – ungodliness; living for God –

---

[1] Because of what follows, I should have put this the other way round: sanctification and antinomianism.

living for self; living under God's word in obedience to Christ – living lawlessly, living without account, just living for self, for the world.

There's much debate these days about antinomianism. And there is much debate about sanctification. And the usual view, the common view, the overwhelmingly-usual view, is that sanctification is by the law. We must look to the law, the ten commandments in particular, 'the moral law' as it's called – it's not called that in Scripture, I might say, but it's called that by the theologians! – the ten commandments are the rule, the standard, and the motive, the spring, to move us to sanctification. As Calvin said – and he formulated the system – as Calvin said: The law is a whip smiting us! We are lazy and we need to be hit into line!' You can read all this in his works. You can read it in my books[2] – my book, in particular, *Christ Is All* – I've given extracts, very fully, proving, showing, demonstrating that Calvin made the whip of the law the great way of sanctification.

Now I turn to this text. Here is Jesus praying for us as believers, and he's praying for our sanctification.

The first thing I would notice about that is this: if Jesus prays for it, then it must be an essential! It must be something vitally important for us. This is no option, believer! We must be sanctified! Now, he's not praying that we'll be separated from the world in justification. He's not praying that we should be separated from the world in regeneration. That's already taken place, earlier in the chapter... he's already said, in John chapter 15 verse 3: 'Now you are clean through the word I have spoken to you', and so on. And all that is complete! What he's praying for here is sanctification in the sense of daily, practical, godly living. And Jesus prays that all his people shall be sanctified.

Believer! It is not an option to live a godly life for Christ and for God! 'Holiness, without which no man shall see the Lord'! And in that passage, if you read it in Hebrews 12, you'll find it's

---

[2] See also the first chapter of this present work.

about sanctification. It's not about the initial, great, secret work of God, when he makes us perfect for ever in Christ! It is our daily living he is talking about there! Holiness, daily, practical, godliness, spirituality of life, obedience to Christ is an essential! Without it, no man shall see the Lord!

I said you're a believer. Well, you're a *professing* believer! But if you're living like the world, you are a worldling! If you are living carnally, you are carnal! You must be sanctified! Jesus prayed for it. It is an essential!

But I say again, Jesus prayed for it! And I make another point from that. It is not only Jesus' desire and earnest prayer – and, therefore, a command to us to be sanctified: 'Be ye holy for I am holy' – if he prays for it, this shows me that this is a fundamental aspect of the *means* of my sanctification! How will I, as a believer, be sanctified? Jesus prays for me to be sanctified! He is ever the same; the same yesterday, today and for ever. He ever lives to make intercession for us. I believe I can overhear him, in his intercession for me now: 'Sanctify them! Sanctify them! Make them holy! You have justified them! O Father, sanctify them!' And this is an essential ingredient in my sanctification: Christ is praying for it for me. And, therefore, seeing he is always heard, I have the help of the Spirit assured to me in this prayer – that I shall be sanctified!

And that takes me on to the Spirit.

'Sanctify them through thy truth' – through your truth – through truth. Now, there is a great deal of debate today about truth versus Spirit; Spirit versus truth; life and Spirit; Spirit and life; word and Spirit; Spirit and word; life and doctrine; life and Scripture. You see, these two are played against each other. *They should never, never, never be played against each other!* It is life *and* Spirit! It is word, truth *and* life! It is Spirit *and* word! It's not either/or! It is both! Sanctify through truth! Truth leads to sanctification. Scripture/obedience linked: life, doctrine, Spirit, word, godliness. All these cluster around each other. They're not either/or's. They make up one whole. We're not sanctified by feelings. We're not sanctified by some mysterious, mystic experience. It is truth and Spirit; it is Spirit and truth: 'Sanctify them through thy truth; your word is truth'. Word and Spirit!

But my main point in this short address is this: What exactly is this truth which is the great means of my sanctification? The truth will not sanctify me on its own – I need the Spirit to enable me to be sanctified. But what is the truth that the Spirit will take me to?

Well, I've already told you what Calvin taught. Calvin said, expressly, it is the law, 'the moral law', the ten commandments. And this acts as not only a standard, but it acts as a whip to drive me to that standard! So he makes *fear* the motive! He makes whip – the whip of the law – the great means of sanctification.

Now what does Christ pray for here? 'Sanctify them through thy law! Thy law is truth'? 'Sanctify them through thy truth! The ten commandments are the truth'?

Now he doesn't say that does he? He says: 'Sanctify them by the truth; your word' – the entire word of God is the truth that sanctifies!

Can you see the contrast here?

Here am I, as a believer. I know, from many scriptures, that it is the Spirit who leads me into sanctification. He leads me to Christ. He shows me Christ. The New Testament is full of this. But how must this be calibrated? How can I find instructions and directions? I'm under law to Christ (Gal. 6:2). 1 Corinthians 9 [verse 21]: 'I am under the law to Christ', 'the law of Christ'. Now where will I find that law written down? OK – the Spirit writes it in my heart! That is the promise of the new covenant. But where will I find it?

Well, I find it in Scripture! But do I find it in the ten commandments? Is that the sum total of it?

Well, the New Testament does use the ten commandments, occasionally – like it uses other things – to give me illustrations, and so on. *But it doesn't take me primarily to the ten commandments*, I assure you. Read the New Testament, and see! And the prayer of Christ here is explicit! 'Sanctify them by the truth; your word' – *the entire word* – 'is truth'.

I would go further!

In the context of John, in the context of the New Testament, I would interpret this to be the entire word of God, *but especially the gospel of our Lord Jesus Christ!* Because it's the *gospel* which is saving! And it's the *gospel* which is sanctifying! I'm reminded of that passage when Paul wrote to Timothy (2 Timothy chapter 3). He urged him to continue in the things that he learned, knowing that *all Scripture* is able to make him wise to salvation. *All Scripture* is profitable: instruction, teaching, conviction, correction, training in righteousness, and so on. The Scriptures! The entire body of the Scriptures is given to instruct us, and to calibrate the Spirit's working within us that we might be sanctified.

But, as I say, primarily – and in the context of Timothy, too, I think you will find it so – it is the gospel of our Lord Jesus Christ which is the prime source of my instruction. I don't mean just the four Gospels. I mean the whole doctrine of the saving work of Christ, as worked out in the New Testament.

Now that's what I see here. I see not that we should be restrained to the ten commandments, and certainly not as a whip! It is the word of God completely. And it's the gospel! It is the good news! Not the whip! It is the love of Christ, the love of God, the mercy of God, the grace of God, the salvation which Christ wrought for us! *This* is the great motive! Indeed, Christ himself! Christ is the gospel! Christ is the gospel, and the gospel is Christ!

It's very interesting to ask Calvin – when he's not talking in his *Institutes* about this system of the law – and to ask him what he thinks this text means. Well, we can ask him! We can ask his view of John 17:17. It's written down. He's published his *Commentary*, and we still have it. Shall I read it to you? Remember he has told us that we are to be sanctified by the ten commandments, and we treat the ten commandments as a whip to smite us into obedience. That's what he says. Now, when he comes to comment on John 17:17, this is what he says:

'The word' here denotes the doctrine of the gospel. True, it is God alone who sanctifies, but as the gospel is the power of God to salvation to everyone that believes (Romans 1:16), whoever departs from the gospel as the means must become more and more filthy and polluted.

Can I read that again?

'The word' here denotes the doctrine of the gospel. True, it is God alone who sanctifies, but as the gospel is the power of God to salvation to everyone that believes (Romans 1:16), whoever departs from the gospel as the means must become more and more filthy and polluted.

I could not agree more with Calvin on this! John Calvin got it dead right here! He says if you want to be an antinomian – 'more and more filthy and polluted' – then give up the gospel, give up the word of God!

So, my friend, if you want to be an antinomian – then reject Scripture! Live as you want! Forget what God has said! Especially forget the gospel! Forget Christ! Live as you want! *But you're on the road to damnation!*

But if you want to be sanctified, then as Calvin said: '"The word" here denotes "the doctrine of the gospel"' – the doctrine, the teaching, of the gospel, the good news of the gospel. And what is the good news of the gospel? The saving work of Christ! The person of Christ! The merit of Christ! True, 'it is God alone who sanctifies', he [Calvin] says, but as 'the gospel is the power' – and I need power to be sanctified, sanctify them through the *power* of your word – 'the power of God to salvation'.

I'm interested in that [statement] by Calvin. He's not just talking about sanctification. He's not just talking about justification. He's talking about *salvation*! Salvation includes the whole lot! So when the Pharisees and the teachers of the law wanted the Christians to go under the law for salvation [Acts 15:1-5], this

48

what they wanted. They wanted Christians to take Calvin's view – as he would later formulate it! Come under the law, they said, and you will be sanctified. As Calvin said: 'No! "The gospel is the power of God salvation to everyone that believes" (and he quotes Romans 1:16). Whoever departs from the gospel as the means' – not only *the standard*, but as *the means* – 'must become more and more filthy and polluted'!

I couldn't agree more with Calvin! *But Calvin didn't agree with himself!*

But, my friend, I'm talking to you. Are you one who has been reared on Calvin's system? – the [his] original system, the law system? Are you finding it a grind? This whip hurts doesn't it? You can't make it, can you? The standard is too high, you can't reach it! It's impossible, isn't it?

You should be looking to Christ! Abundance of scriptures show it: 'Consider him! Set your affections on him'!

'But all this must be calibrated!'

I fully agree! And that's why I'm speaking to you now! The Scriptures are your calibration – not just the ten commandments! Go to the entire range of Scripture! And look for Christ everywhere. Luke 24, as he spoke to his disciples, Christ said: 'Christ is in *all* the Scriptures'. And beginning with Moses and the prophets, he revealed himself to his disciples. And that's what you must look for! Wherever you open your Bible – law, prophets, psalms, the Gospels, the letters, the prophetical bits, the poetical bits, the historical portions, whatever – look for Jesus. Jesus is in all the Scriptures. Set your affections upon him, and you will be sanctified as you grow in the likeness of the Christ you see revealed in Scripture. Look for Jesus! 'Sir', said the Greeks, 'we would see Jesus'!

And *that's* what Jesus is praying for here: 'Sanctify them', he says. 'Take the whole of Scripture! May they be subservient to Scripture! May they be submissive to Scripture! May they bow to Scripture! And may the Spirit help them, and lead them to me, so that looking upon me, and gazing upon me, and walking with me, and talking with me, I will pray for them, and so they will be sanctified'!

'The gospel', as Calvin said – and I agree – 'is the power of God unto salvation' – in this respect: it is the *means* of sanctification. If you would be more and more filthy and polluted, my friend, then leave Christ, leave the gospel. But if you would be sanctified, if you would be saved, look to Jesus!

Indeed, I go on just to finish with this: if you are an unbeliever, the word of God tells me you are a sinner, and on the road to damnation, you're under the wrath of God – now! But it also tells me that if you believe on the Lord Jesus Christ, if you look to him, if you call upon his name, if you repent of your sins and turn to him, you will be saved!

But my final word will be for all of us who are believers: Jesus prayed for us. He's praying for us now my brothers and sisters. Let us fall in with this. Let us take our Bibles – *all* our Bibles – looking for Christ in the Scriptures, looking to be like him, and grow like him, and to be sanctified in this present evil age. 'Sanctify them', he prays to his Father. 'Sanctify them by the truth; your word is truth'. And Christ, being the word of God, is *the* truth we must concentrate upon, above all. Look to Jesus, Jesus Christ the Lord.

# Antinomianism: Hope Is The Answer

*How great is the love the Father has lavished on us, that we should be called children of God! And that is what we are! The reason the world does not know us is that it did not know him. Dear friends, now we are children of God, and what we will be has not yet been made known. But we know that when he appears, we shall be like him, for we shall see him as he is. Everyone who has this hope in him purifies himself, just as he is pure. Everyone who sins breaks the law; in fact, sin is lawlessness. But you know that he appeared so that he might take away our sins. And in him is no sin (1 John 3:1-5).*

I would like to speak to you for a few minutes on 1 John chapter 3 and verse 3; 1 John, the third chapter and the third verse: 'Everyone who has this hope in him purifies himself, just as he is pure'; 'everyone who has this hope in him purifies himself, just as he is pure'.

Let me explain the words at the moment, the first part: 'everyone'. Now who is this 'everyone' that John is talking to, and talking about ? Well, let's start at verse 1: 'How great is the love the Father has lavished on us, that we should be called children of God! And that is what we are!' Verse 2: 'Dear friends, now we are children of God'. 'Everyone' in this context, then, in verse 3, 'everyone' is all the children of God; in other words, true believers. And if we go over the entire letter, we shall soon find that John means those who have a living faith in the Lord Jesus Christ: they have turned from their sins; they have trusted Christ; they are washed in his precious blood; they are clothed in his righteousness; they are anointed by the Spirit; they are the children of God; they are justified, washed, cleansed from all their sins; they have the inward working of God's Spirit; they belong to God; they are adopted; they are the children of God. So John is saying, in verse 3, 'all true believers', every man, every woman who has this hope in him.

Now, who is the 'him'? Clearly, in the context, it is the Lord Jesus Christ; God in Christ.

If you look at the entire letter, you can see this is what John means: 'Everyone, every true believer who has this hope in the Lord Jesus Christ purifies himself, even as he is pure, just as he is pure. Just as Christ is, so the believer must purify himself and be like Christ'.

So, John is telling believers their responsibility. He's reminded them of their privileges, but now he is telling them that their responsibility is: You must purify yourself.

Now we mustn't get the wrong impression, the wrong end of the stick here. He (John) doesn't mean that we as believers, that believers have this power in themselves to purify themselves. He is telling us our responsibility as believers. He has explained that the Spirit only, Christ only, the energy of God's Spirit, can enable us to live to the glory of God. We have an anointing from the Holy One – in the previous chapter, he explains; and so on. But, nevertheless, John is saying quite clearly, that the responsibility of every believer is to purify him or herself, and to live in this present carnal, evil age as Christ would live.

Now I'm talking to whom... I don't know, do I? I'm just speaking, but you're listening to me. Are you a believer in our Lord Jesus Christ? Are you trusting him as your Saviour, your Lord, your King? Very well! Then I am speaking to you. John is speaking to you. And this is what he says to you my brother and my sister – and he says it to me. He says you as a believer, you must purify yourself, now in this present evil age, you must live as Christ would live. That is your responsibility. That is your duty. That is the commandment I give upon you, and put before you. Purify yourself!

I know there are many people who think that they can live what they call as 'a carnal Christian'. They are grossly mistaken! There *is* a text in 1 Corinthians about that, but Paul is rebuking the Corinthians: he is not allowing them to be carnal! As a believer, my friend, you cannot live as the world lives. You cannot live as a carnal man, or a carnal woman. You have to purify yourself – even Christ is pure. 'Be holy for I am holy', says God. Now *that* is the commandment; that is your responsibility.

The truth is, everybody who thinks about this subject is seriously, is really, probably, agreed at this stage. There are those, of course, who think they can live carnally. As I said, they are mistaken!

Now let me turn to the rest of us. We know that we have to live as a godly man, or a godly woman, in this present evil age. Very well! The great question is: What is the standard? And the even greater question is: How can I reach that standard? What is the motive to drive me to that? What is going to give me energy and the will and the desire to live to that standard?

Now this is where believers radically divide! The vast majority of believers, Reformed and evangelical believers – what do they think? Whether they know it, or whether they don't know it, they follow John Calvin. And he taught that it is the law of God – the ten commandments, he restricted it to, the ten commandments – that's the standard! And the ten commandments are the driver. He said the ten commandments, the law, is a whip to whack us, to smite us, because we're lazy – lazy donkeys, he said, and we need whipping to obey the law, and that will make us keep the law, and so we will purify ourselves, and be purified in God's sight. That's what John Calvin said.[1] And that's what the majority of believers think.

---

[1] I do not mean in his *Commentaries*, but in his *Institutes* – which, as he told us, are to be taken as his definitive work. In his *Commentary*, he said this: The apostle 'now draws this inference, that the desire for holiness should not grow cold in us, because our happiness has not as yet appeared, for that hope is sufficient; and we know that what is hoped for is as yet hid. The meaning then is, that though we have not Christ now present before our eyes, yet if we hope in him, it cannot be but that this hope will excite and stimulate us to follow purity, for it leads us straight to Christ, whom we know to be a perfect pattern of purity'. As you can see, Calvin here contradicted what he said in his *Institutes*. Sadly, it is his *Institutes* which (as he wanted) have dominated Reformed and evangelical theology and practice in this vital area.

They think that by looking at the standard of the law, trying to keep the law, and be whipped by the law when they transgress – fear, punishment, guilt, keeping rules, keeping regulations – this will enable them to live in this present evil age.

I know the creeds say that. I know the great Confessions say it. I know the pastors and the teachers say it. I know the writers write it. I know the systematic theology's say it. I know! I know!

But I ask you, in these few minutes, look at what John says. 'John, you tell me!' 'I *have* told you! He says. Read it again! 1 John 3:3: 'Everyone who has this hope in Christ purifies himself, just as he is pure'. First the standard: 'Just as Christ is pure'! Do you want to know the standard of holiness? Do you want to know the standard of godliness to reach? Look at Christ! 'As *he* is pure'! How would Christ live, here, now? What would Christ say in this situation? What would Christ do? What would Christ think? How would Christ react?

Now how can I find that out? By reading his word: 'Sanctify them through your truth; your word is truth'! That was how he prayed. 'All Scripture is given by inspiration of God, and is profitable' – and I'll summarise it – for sanctification. It's profitable for *salvation*, but it's profitable for *sanctification*! So we look in the Scriptures, and we're looking for Christ. And as we see Christ – how he reacted, how he lived, how he spoke – so we must purify ourselves, and by God's Spirit, keep Christ in our mind. Keep thinking of what he would do, how he would react, and what he would say. That is the standard!

But even more important, even more pressing is: How can I reach that standard? And John tells me that too: 'Everyone who has *this* hope in him purifies himself, just as he is pure'. 'Has this hope in him'! Now 'hope' in the New Testament does not mean 'cross your fingers and hope for the best!' It means 'confident expectation, the certain, sure, guaranteed expectation'. Now *what* guaranteed expectation, what sure thing, have we got in Christ?

Well, I'll tell you some of the things that John has told us – and some of the things in other Scriptures: Jesus' blood has washed from all our sins; Jesus has sent his Spirit into our hearts; he has adopted us to be his children; he has anointed us with the Spirit; he has given us the witness of his Spirit within our spirits that we are the children of God; he has set his love upon us; he guarantees to keep us, and to pray for us without ceasing, and to come again and receive us to himself, and to change us. Indeed, John says here, one day he will come back for us, and he will purify us, and 'we shall be like him, for we shall see him as he is'. We shall see the Lord Jesus again; he will come back for us; he will change us to be like him; and we shall be with him and like him for ever.

'Everyone who has this hope' – the forgiveness of their sins, the assurance of everlasting life, and the certainty that one day we shall see and be like *Christ* – 'everyone who has this hope in him purifies himself, even as Jesus is pure'. *There* is the motive! It is Christ, Christ, Christ! It's what God has done in Christ, what God is doing in Christ, what God will do for us in Christ. Christ living for us now – having come for us, and died for us – living for us now, coming again for us. Jesus! Jesus! Jesus!

Set your mind upon him! Set your affections upon him! This what John, in effect, is saying. Think about the glories to come! Think about Christ! Think about the standard. but here is the motive! The motive and the standard are one: it is Christ!

I'm not making it up, am I? Be honest! Look at what John says. Read it for yourself! Think about what Calvin and the majority of teachers say: Law! Law! Law! And listen to John: Christ! Christ! Christ! Law? Law? Law? Grace! Grace! Grace! That is what John says! And that is what he means! There's not an atom of law is there? It's all of grace!

The answer to antinomianism – which is living carnally – is not law! It is Christ! It is grace! The great means, and the great motive, and the great standard, of sanctification is not law, law, law. It is grace, grace, grace! Above all, it is Christ! There isn't an atom of law here!

'Ah!' says an objector, 'you read on... verse 4: "Everyone who sins breaks the law"! In fact, sin is lawlessness. You see, there's the law!'

I quite agree, my friend. I quite agree. But does it say that the law is my standard? Does it say the law is my spur? No? It doesn't say anything of the sort! And look what it does go on to say, verse 5: 'But you know that he appeared' – Christ again! – 'so that he might take away our sins. And in him is no sin. And no one who lives in him keeps on sinning'. You see, immediately, I mean, I agree with you, John has mentioned the law here. Sin is lawlessness, yes, lawlessness is sin. I quite agree! But the motive and the means and the spur of our sanctification is all of Christ, is it not? The context says it. John says it bluntly, plainly: 'Everyone' – without exception – 'who has this hope in *Christ* purifies himself, just as he is pure'.

Calvin is wrong! The Confessions are wrong on this point! The systematic theology's are wrong on this point! The 'great men' are wrong! The pastors and teachers are wrong. John is telling us! It is Christ! Christ! Christ!

And if there is an unbeliever listening to me, if you've got this far: you need salvation! And, you know, it's the same answer for you, needing *salvation*, as it is for the believer needing *sanctification*! To be saved, go to Jesus: 'Believe on the Lord Jesus Christ and you will be saved'. Leave aside your rites and ceremonies, works, pastors, priests, churches, and all – go to Christ, trust Christ!

But I come back to the main point: What is the answer to antinomianism? What is the great motive, means and standard of sanctification? 'Everyone' – who is a Christian, a believer, man and woman, everyone of us – you my friend, and I myself – I'm speaking to you now: We must purify ourselves. What is the standard? It is Jesus. And what is the means and motive stirring us for this, and stirring driver for this? It is Christ! Think upon Christ! Look to Christ! And may Christ get all the glory from our poor feeble lives.

# Christ, Not Law, Banishes Fear

*Who will bring any charge against those whom God has chosen? It is God who justifies. Who is he that condemns? Christ Jesus, who died – more than that, who was raised to life – is at the right hand of God and is also interceding for us (Rom. 8:33-34).*

I would like to have a few words with you on a very important subject. I'm addressing true believers – those who know the Lord Jesus Christ as their Lord and Saviour. They have trusted him, relied upon him, called upon him for salvation. He has forgiven their sins, washed them in his blood, and they have peace with God. I'm speaking to you, my friend, if you're in that condition; you're a believer.

May I ask you how it is with your soul at this time?

I'm afraid that many believers, if they were honest, would have to say something along the lines that as they look at their own spiritual condition, as they measure their own spiritual state, and then they look at the Scriptures, they see a large gap between what the New Testament believers seemed to enjoy and what they themselves are enjoying – or lacking in enjoyment – in their own personal experience at this time!

What do I mean? In the New Testament, they see believers who can speak in terms like this: having joy inexpressible and full of glory. They read of believers, of whom it's said that they have glory, a sense of glory, and *ever-increasing* glory. They read of believers of whom it's said that they have *liberty*, and this sense of liberty, and they rejoice in this with joy inexpressible, hope, confidence, glory, liberty. I am, of course, referring to texts such as 1 Peter 1, 2 Corinthians 3, Galatians 5; and so on, and so on, and so on. And I'm sure that many believers, reading such texts of Scripture as this, such passages, they say to themselves: 'Well, I'm not having that! In fact, I feel that my experience is dry, barren, arid! I seem to be going through the Christian life by rote, as it were, by rule, and regulation, and form. It doesn't seem to be a living, vital, joyous, triumphant experience. And yet I see in the New Testament, quite clearly, that the early believers had *this* sense of liberty, and confidence and assurance. And I don't have it! I'm afraid, I feel I'm in some sort of bondage. And yet I read that we're not given the spirit of bondage! We don't have a spirit of fear. And yet I do!'

Can I say something to help you my friend? Well, not me! I can't say it! I can mouth the words, but I'm going to say all I say from a passage of Scripture. And my passage that I've chosen to speak to you about is Romans chapter 8. And I want to raise two points with you from verses 33 and 34; Romans chapter 8, and verses 33 and 34. It's two questions. The apostle asks two questions here. If you look at Paul, you will see that, well in company with Christ and many other teachers and preachers in the Bible, they use the more powerful way of teaching: that is, by questions, and not simply by statements. Statements – which we get a lot of today in preaching – is a very bland way of teaching. The apostle's way is very often to raise questions. And not closed questions – with the answer 'Yes!' or 'No!' But with open answers, open questions – and you have to fill in the details. And he does it here – verse 33: 'Who will bring any charge against those whom God has chosen?' And in verse 34: 'Who is he that condemns?

Now these questions are rhetorical; that is to say, the answer is completely understood. The truth is, in a very real and fundamental sense, *nobody* can lay *any* charge or make *any* condemnation against any child of God! That is true! But the way the apostle goes on, and the whole context of these two questions, shows that he knows that believers *do* have this sense of condemnation, and *do* have this sense of criticism and accusation against them! And they do have a sense, therefore, of lacking joy, and happiness, and assurance, and freedom which the believer should have. And that's why he asks these questions.

You may say: 'Well these are not my questions!'

You wait! Perhaps I can say something that might help you here. I will tell you who might accuse you, who might criticise you, who might point the finger at you.

Well, I will tell you one for start: Satan! Satan knows where you live, my brother and sister! He knows your weak points. Above all, he knows your strong points! And he knows how to tempt you, and twist arguments, and point the finger at you, especially – if you know anything of this – in the small hours! He knows how to open up your conscience, and remind you of your sins, and accuse you. And this can send you into a spiral, downward, a vortex, where you feel that you have failed, and you have to confess it. And you begin to feel the shame of it, the embarrassment of it. And you begin to lose your joy. Satan has gained a victory over you.

The world can do it! It's very prone to do it – calling us hypocrites. And, of course, my friends, I have to admit, with you, we're all sinners, and the world can find places where they can touch us, and point the finger at us. But this sometimes goes home, and pierces us, and gives us a sense of fear, and doubt, lack of assurance. And we have to admit the force of what the world is saying against us. And so we get again into this spiral downwards!

Our own conscience, our own flesh, can rise against us, and remind us of how we've fallen, how we've failed, how we've stumbled, how we've sinned, how we've come short! The weakness of our service! The coldness of our hearts! And again we go down into this spiral, and this treadmill of never breaking free of worry and anxiety, and lack of joy. And we come into fear, and timidity, and dryness, and darkness.

And, of course, the church can do it! Our teachers can do it! The books we read can do it! They tell us these – certain – things, and we feel the guilt of it; and so on. Again we get into the state of bondage!

Now, what does Paul mean [teach] here? What can I say from this – Romans chapter 8 verses 33 and 34? You must remember that these verses just don't appear out of a blue sky! They've come in chapter 8, which follows on from chapter 7, and 6, and so on. So let's just remind ourselves of where we've reached in this letter so far, what Paul has established. Has he not proved to us – as we've read it, if you read it through, if you've not read it lately, read it again – has he not proved to us, that though we are sinners under the wrath of God – chapters 3 and 4 and 5 – Christ has died for us, propitiated the wrath of God, appeased the wrath of God, borne it for us, and we are washed from our sins? Have we not read, in chapter 5, that he has made us completely righteous and justified in [God's] Son? In chapters 6 and 7, has he not reminded us, and taught us, and explained to us, that when we came to Christ, we were united to him, we died with him, and we rose with him? We are no longer under the law, the law is no longer our slave master, the law is no longer our husband? We are under a new slave master Christ, and we are married to a new husband – Christ – that we might bear fruit for him?

So we've come to chapter 8, verse 1: 'Therefore, there is now no condemnation to those who are in Christ Jesus, because through Christ Jesus the law the Spirit of life set me free from the law of sin and death. For what the law was powerless to do in that it was weakened by the flesh, God did by sending his own Son in the likeness of sinful man' and 'to be a sin offering' – an offering for sin, to be made sin for us 'in order' – and he condemns sin in man – 'in order that the righteous requirements of the law might be fully met in us'; and so on, and so on. And yet, having said all that – and we go on in chapter 8, about verse 16, for example: 'The Spirit himself' bears witness – 'testifies with our spirit that we are God's children' – are children of God. And yet, even so, we have fear! As he says in verse 15: 'You did not receive a spirit that makes you a slave again to fear, but you received the Spirit of sonship'. And yet we have to confess, very often, many of us, that we *do* have a spirit of fear! We *do* have a spirit of bondage! And we *don't* have this sense of assurance, and this sense of confidence!

What's happened?

Well, we've fixed our eyes on the wrong object!

It could be that we've fixed our eyes upon our works, instead of Christ, over the matter of justification. Have you done that, my friend? Has the devil told you about your sins, and you begin to think: Well, I'm not right with God, then? You're right with God by your works! You're right with God by Christ's works, and your trust in Christ! Christ has perfected you forever, Hebrews 10! The blood of Christ has washed you from *all* sin! You're without spot, or wrinkle, or stain, or any such thing! I'm quoting various Scriptures to you. And I remind you again of Romans 8:1: 'There is no condemnation to you'. Now, stop looking at your works! Stop looking at the law, and saying: Now if I try and keep that, I'll be right! The devil's taking you to look at the law instead of Christ! Look to Christ for your justification, again! Remind yourself: 'It is Christ who died – yea, rather who risen again! And I'm justified! There is no condemnation to me!' This is what Paul says in our verses: 'Who will bring any charges against those whom God has chosen? It is God who justifies'. Your works didn't justify you in the beginning! They won't justify you now! You're justified, anyway! Perfectly, forever! Remind yourself of it! It is Christ Jesus who died!

But I more particularly want to home in on this: I feel that many believers have gone wrong in this matter, and got a lack of assurance and come into fear and bondage, because of the second aspect of this work – [wrong on] the [teaching of] Romans 6 and 7. They have been taught by their teachers that they are to go back under the law for sanctification. Now is this *your* problem, my friend? Are you looking at your works for sanctification? Are you looking to see what you're doing, how far you've attained? Are you looking at the law, the rules and regulations, the commandments – thou shall not do this! – and you're striving to do it, you're tightening your belt? And what do you see? You see you're failing. And what does this do for you? It gets you into a spiral – downward – of fear, and bondage, trying harder, and failing all the time. You lack assurance. And all the sense of joy – an inexpressible joy and glory – it's just gone out of the window, hasn't it?

Well, your teachers were wrong when they told you to go under law for sanctification! Read again Romans 6 and 7. Read it out loud, slowly! Read it in other versions to the one you're used to! Read it out loud, slowly, I say again. Let the argument sink in! Don't put any glosses on the words! You're not under the law! You're free! You're not sanctified by the law! You're sanctified by Christ! Read it and see! You're married to Christ! You've died to the law – don't go back to your old marriage with the law! Don't go back to the law for justification! And certainly – Romans 6 and 7 – don't go back to it for sanctification!

'The law of the Spirit of life has set me free from the law sin and death'! In Christ Jesus, God has set me free from the law of sin and death for justification, *and for sanctification!* And he *is* talking about sanctification when he gets there into Romans 8:1 and on! As he says: 'In order that the righteous requirements of the law might be fully met in us, who do not live according to the flesh but according to the Spirit'.

So where does all this fear come from? And all this doubt? It's because you're looking at your works for assurance, you're looking at your works for sanctification! You're looking at law keeping!

What is the answer that Paul has to these criticisms and accusations?

My text again! Verses 33 and 34 of Romans 8: 'Who will bring any charge against those whom God has chosen?' Will you do it yourself? Will your teachers do it? Will the devil do it? Will the church do it? 'Who is he that condemns?' Now what is his answer? 'Christ Jesus'! Notice the dramatic Greek there. You can't see the Greek, but the English is: 'Christ Jesus'! It is dramatic like that: 'Christ Jesus, who died'! He doesn't say: 'It is Christ Jesus'. He says just: 'Christ Jesus'! Christ is the answer!

So what should you be doing, my friend? Stop looking at the law for assurance! Stop looking at the law and your works for sanctification! Of course, there is a place for this – 1 John, and so on – but where should your eye primarily be fixed? Fix your eyes on Jesus! I'm not making it up! 'Christ Jesus, who died – more than that, who was raised to life – is at the right hand of

God and is also interceding for us'. Set your mind, set your affection, upon Christ! Look to him! 'Come unto me', he says, 'and I will give you rest'. Don't go to the law! Come to me, he says. Don't go to the law for justification.

'Well', the teachers say, 'that's right!' 'But', they say, 'you must go to the law for sanctification'. No! 'Come to *me*', says Jesus. Come to *me* – for sanctification as well as justification! And that's what Paul says here: 'It is God who justifies. It is Christ who died, who is raised, living, praying for me, interceding'. Are you fearful that you will fall, stumble and fall away? Christ will intercede for you! Christ will keep you! Christ is coming again! Christ died for you! Look to Christ! And this is the way of sanctification – not to the law! Look to Christ! Christ is your deliver! Do you want this liberty and joy? Then set your affection, your mind, and your heart upon Christ!

Of course your sanctification is feeble. Of course your sanctification is below standard. We confess it. Let's confess it! I'm not belittling it! It's true! But look at Christ! Never man spoke like this man! Never man lived like this man! There is no Saviour like Christ! Look to Christ! This is the answer to all fear! This is the answer to lack of assurance! This is the answer to doubts! This is the answer to all questions! I can't answer the questions – Christ can! I have my doubts – there is no doubt with Christ! My works are feeble – Christ's are perfect! Look to Jesus! That is what Paul is saying here!

Let me take just one more moment or two to prove it to you.

Whatever you make of Romans 7, the last part of it – and we all have difficulties with Romans 7, the last part, and I'm not going to get involved in those difficulties here – I just want to pick on verses 24 and 25. Now, whatever interpretation or understanding you have of this passage, these words resonate, don't they? They ring a bell, don't they? They're chiming in exactly with what I've just said. What have I just said? Do you lack assurance? Look to Christ! Do you want to be sanctified? Look to Christ! Law? Law? No! Christ! Christ!

What does Paul say in Romans 7:24 and 25? 'What a wretched man I am! Who will rescue me from this body of death?' Do you sympathise with him? Do you empathise with him? Do you know what he's talking about? Do you feel at the moment – believer, I'm talking to you – do you feel wretched, depressed, low, doubting, fearful, questioning all these things? You lack the joy you should have? What does Paul say? 'What a wretched man that I am! Who will rescue me?'

What is his answer? Verse 25! 'Thanks be to God – through Jesus Christ our Lord!'

Can you see that is the truth? It's not *my* counsel! It's not *my* teaching! I know I'm going against the Reformed teaching and the evangelical teaching, the great mass of the teachers, I know I'm going against them! But is it not true what I've just said to you? Is it not scriptural? Is it not what Paul said? What's the answer to all his fears, all his doubts, all his sins, all his sorrows? What's the answer to the question: How can I be assured? How can I be sanctified? Is the answer not always: 'Christ, Christ Jesus our Lord'?

If there's an unbeliever listening to me [or reading this], the answer is the same for you. We came this way when we were justified. We looked to Christ. If you look to Christ, you will be saved. If you look at sacraments, or ceremonies, priests, or church, or pastors, or parents, or whatever it might be, you will fail, miserably! But – if you look to Jesus Christ, you will be saved. Now, and forever!

But I come back to you, believer. I set out in this little talk to help you, to help myself, to get to this assurance, an unspeakable joy, full of glory, ever-increasing glory, this sense of liberty. And you won't find that by looking at the law! You won't find that by looking at yourself! You will find it only by looking to Christ! But if you look to Christ, and take him to be all in all, all these other things will fall into place. Your doubts and fears will melt away. They'll never be gone completely in this life, I know – that will have to wait to eternal glory – but as you look to Christ, you will grow increasingly in this unspeakable joy and full of glory, here and now.

So, look to Jesus Christ our Lord!

# Antinomianism: Peter's Answer To It

I would like to speak to you for a few minutes on 1 Peter, chapter 4, and verses 1 to 5; 1 Peter, chapter 4, verses 1 to 5:

*Therefore, since Christ suffered in his body, arm yourselves also with the same attitude, because he who has suffered in his body is done with sin. As a result, he does not live the rest of his earthly life for evil human desires, but rather for the will of God. For you have spent enough time in the past doing what pagans choose to do – living in debauchery, lust, drunkenness, orgies, carousing and detestable idolatry. They think it strange that you do not plunge with them into the same flood of dissipation, and they heap abuse on you. But they will have to give account to him who is ready to judge the living and the dead (1 Pet. 4:1-5).*

I want to have a few words with you on this subject of antinomianism. Do you know what antinomianism is? Do you know how to recognise it? You may have heard about it, and you may have heard it is 'a bad thing'. I say again: Do you know what it is? And how will you recognise it?

Let me say straightaway, like Peter, writing here, I am speaking, in the first instance, to those of you who are believers. Peter says in verse 3: 'You used to be pagans; this is what you used to do; you were a pagan'. Obviously, they've been converted, and they're now believers. So, in the first instance, I'm speaking to those of you who have a living faith in the Lord Jesus Christ, and you know him as your Saviour and Lord.

Now then, I want to talk to about antinomianism.

Well, there are two things I want to say about it. First of all, we should think about the theory behind it – the principles underlying, the doctrine, if you like, of antinomianism, the theory. And then there is the practice, the outworking, the practical effects, the consequences, the visible signs of antinomianism.

Now, the cause, the basis, the doctrine of antinomianism, comes from these two Greek words: *anti* and *nomos* – 'against law'.

And, literally, an antinomian is one who will not have any law to govern him. If you like, he is a law unto himself. He is lawless, and he wants to live the way he wants, and nobody and nothing is going to impose any rule on him! He is going to live as he wants! His 'rule', if you like, is: 'I do as I please!' Anti-law!

It is the consequences that most people are concerned with. The consequences, I think, can be easily described, simply described, in our passage, in verse 3. This is what Peter says: Pagans! Living as pagans, such as this: 'debauchery, lust, drunkenness, orgies, carousing, detestable idolatry'; or, as he goes on, 'flood of dissipation'. I think that fairly sums it up. The antinomianism we are talking about is living as a pagan: I see it, I want it, I have it – pleasure, sex, power, money, self, living for this life – let us eat and drink and be merry! Living as I want to do! Living as pleases me! Living for the body! Living for the here and now!

Peter says: 'This is how you used to live!' Paul, writing to the Corinthians, says: 'This is how you used to live!' Writing to the Romans, he describes – in the first chapters – how the pagans live: in all manner of evil and wickedness and sin, living for self, all sexual perversions, entertainment, all sorts of gods and practices, and experiences which they have to gratify themselves, here and now.

Most believers are convinced from Scripture, and by experience, and by inward testimony, that to live like that – as a believer – is quite wrong, sinful. There may be some – there have been in the past, and there may be some now – who think that marks like this – drunkenness, orgies, carousing, paganism – is a mark of the highest grace. I can say what I think about that very simply: it's abominable! If you are like that, my friend – anybody who's listening to me – then my text for you is in Hebrews 12 and verse 14: 'Holiness, without which no man shall see the Lord!' And don't hide away from that text by saying: Oh! that means justification: that's how God sees me! The writer of Hebrews – in Hebrews 12 – you read it for yourself – you will see – is talking about practical holiness, practical godliness. And if you live like pagans, you are a pagan, and you're not a believer! Have I said it plain enough?

But my concern is not mainly with that class of person. There are very few of those, I hope. But the vast majority of believers, the overwhelming majority of believers – we know, don't we, that we must not live as the pagans do. The great issue is – we're persuaded of *that* – the great issue is: How can I live as a Christian should live? What is the Christian life? And how can I produce it?

What is the Christian life? The opposite of these things! I think I can sum it up quite simply: it is that they would live as Jesus would live! God – Romans 8 – has chosen us, and called us and brought us to Christ, that he might bring us increasingly into conformity to Christ. And one day – 1 John 3 tells us – we shall see him, and we shall be like him, for we shall see him as he is, and we shall be like him forever. God's intention is to make us Christ-like. So the life I must live now is summed up like this: How would Jesus live here? What would he say? What would he think? What would he do? Where would he go? Let me be like Christ!

Now I don't think there's any issue, really, with this. I think we're all on the same page here. The great question is, as I say: How can we get there?

Most teachers and preachers, most church leaders, and writers on these subjects, have one recipe for it. And it virtually is a recipe! 'You live according to these rules! I'm going to give you some rules, and I'm going to set these rules before you. You keep these rules and regulations in your mind! And you keep them, and you will live the life that pleases God!' They usually argue for the ten commandments – in theory – but they usually add a host of other rules – man-made rules – which they impose upon you. And you do it for yourself, as well! You do it by rule and by rote: You must not do this! You must do the other! You must be regular in this habit! You must avoid that! And this kind of approach.

Does it work? Yes! That's what most people would say. Many pastors would say they can look out on their congregation, and they can see those who are doing the right thing, and are living this life: they're wearing the right clothes; they're in the right place; they've got the right family-life, the right home-life. They seem to be doing it! It all seems to be right! They (the pastors) can recognise it.

Or so they think!

But they're dreadfully wrong! Because all they're doing is looking at the outward appearance! As we know, man looks at the outward appearance, but God looks on the heart. And what God wants from me is not simply outward conformity to certain rules. He wants an inward, heart, experience: 'My son! Give me your heart!' Man looks on the outward appearance: God looks on the heart! How can I get *heart* Christ-likeness?

You see, the trouble with the rule-and-conformity method is it tries to work into the heart from the outside. But the risk is it produces a load of legal, cardboard cut-outs, look-alikes: conformists to the rules that are laid before the people.

If you're doing it, my friend, how do you find it? It's a struggle, isn't it? For *fear* is at the bottom! You know that! You *fear* to do this! You *fear* to do that! You're afraid when you do! You feel guilty for doing these things! And the pressure upon you for these rules and regulations... and you find it a struggle, don't you? And you know, although you're outwardly conforming, you feel often that you are dry and arid, and, maybe, even resentful, inside.

You know the story of the boy, the little boy, who was taken to the meeting with his father, and at one place they had to stand in the meeting. And the boy didn't want to stand, and the father insisted that his boy should stand. And, of course, he did stand. But this is what the boy said: 'I'm standing outside; but I'm still sitting inside!'

And you know the trouble with law? In my country, we have speeding limits. They're supposed to be the maximum. Most people treat them as the minimum. I know from experience that when our Chancellor of the Exchequer produces a budget, and gives the regime for the income tax for the coming year, accountants are sitting up all night preparing reports for their clients to tell them how they should best manage their financial affairs in the coming year to minimise their taxes. I'm not saying there's anything wrong with it. All I'm saying to you, instinctively, when a law is passed, the instinct is: How can I get round it?

Try this experiment. Put a child in a room, and say: 'You can open every cupboard *but* that one there; every drawer but that one there!' Go out of the room. What will happen? You know what will happen: the child will open the drawer!

The law does not produce grace! The law does not produce Christ-likeness! Rules and regulations do not work!

I'm not talking to you about my opinion! Look at what Peter says: 'I want you', he says, 'you must not live as pagans do!' Now let's just see! Find the word 'law' in this passage! I can't see it! He gives me commandments, I'm not saying that [he doesn't], that's not what I'm saying. But the commandments are what I can't do! What's his motive? What's his argument? That's what I want! 'Peter! Tell me the reasoning behind this approach to Christ-likeness! How can I reach it?'

Well, he gives me the argument. Let me read it to you: 'Therefore (verse 1), since Christ suffered in his body, arm yourselves also with the same attitude, because he who has suffered in his body is done with sin. As a result, he does not live the rest of his earthly life for evil human desires'; and so on. Can you see: if you get verse 1 right – then verse 2, as a result, you will not live in this pagan way; you will live as Christ.

And what is his argument? Keep these rules! I'll smite you if you don't keep these rules! The law is iron. Calvin called it 'a whip'! Is that what Peter says? No! What does he say?

Notice he talks of Christ! There's a *big* difference! We should be *gospel* preachers; those of us who preach – we should be

71

*gospel* preachers, not *legal* preachers! We shouldn't be preaching law; we should preach Christ! That is what Peter did here: 'Therefore, since Christ suffered in his body, arm yourselves also with the same attitude'. He's after their minds, their thinking. He's not after their conformity. He doesn't aim for conformity. He aims for their thinking. And he knows that once he's got their thinking right, this will come into their heart, and once it has come to their heart, then it will come into their lives. Romans 6:17 says this: the mind, and then the heart, and the will, and the life.

What is his argument? Christ suffered in his body. Arm yourselves also with the same attitude. Think of Christ's suffering in his body! 'Because he who has suffered in his body is done with sin'.

What does 'suffered in his body – done with sin' mean? Well, you suffer in your body, when you get the 'flu; you suffer in your body, when you're cold; you suffer in the body, when you get tired; you suffer in the body, when you're poor; you suffer in the body, when you're hungry; you suffer in the body, when you get cancer. Does it mean when people get cancer, and they're hungry, and they're cold, they don't sin? As a result, he does not live the rest of his life for sins? Because he has suffered in his body, he is done with sin?

Of course not! When Peter says 'suffered in his body', here, he clearly means 'dead', 'has died'. You can offer all the temptations you like to a corpse, you can make it as attractive as you like to a corpse, and you will never get a corpse to sin! Why? Because the corpse is dead! 'Therefore, since Christ died. arm yourselves with the same attitude, because he who has died is done with sin. As a result, he does not live the rest of his life for the pagan's way as he used to'.

So, what is Peter's way of answering antinomianism?

Look to Christ! Set your mind upon Christ! Particularly his death, particularly his blood shed on the cross. Why? Well, think of him, as your Saviour – dying for you, my friend. I'm speaking to you as a believer: think of him, dying for you, shedding his blood. And as you think upon him – when the temptations come, the thought of Christ dying for you will guard you, arm you in your mind – that's Peter's words – arm you, help you to think right. Arm yourselves with the same attitude! Did Christ die for me? How can I sin against him? He loved me: how can I sin against this love?

But it is more than that. It's more than Christ died for me.

Romans 6! And I think 1 Peter 4 is a parallel passage to Romans 6. When Christ died, we who are believers were united to him, so when he died, we died; when he was buried, we were buried; when he rose, we rose. We died with Christ, and in Christ!

So arm yourselves with this mind! Christ died on the cross: I died with him! I am crucified with him! All his benefits, all his works and merits are mine! He died to give them to me. I am in him! How can I sin?

It's not only: How can I sin! The thought the more I concentrate upon Christ, the less sin will be attractive to me. I shall be armed in my attitude, in my mind, by dwelling on the fact that I died with Christ, how can I sin! Why should I sin! Why will I sin! I'd rather live for Jesus – he who lived and died for me!

Law? If you read on in Romans 6, and into Romans 7, you will get the same teaching as you get here, more fully explained. And what is that? The law will not sanctify you, my friend! In fact, Romans 7 says this – and Romans 6, as a matter of fact – you have to be dead to the law to be alive to God – to be able to live a sanctified life! Rules will not sanctify you! It is Christ, his blood and righteousness, his death for you, and you in him! He is in you, and you are in him!

So, would you be free from antinomianism! Then think of Christ! Set your heart and your mind upon Christ! Think of him dying *for* you, and *living* for you! Think of him dying in your place, and coming again for you! And think of the fact that you *died* in him to sin, to law and to death, and you're alive in him, and seated with him now in everlasting glory. And I assure you – not me assuring you, really – it's Peter! 'As a result', he says (verse 2), 'this will enable you, as a result, if you arm yourselves in your thinking – with this mind – you will not live the rest of your earthly life for evil human desires'!

Am I speaking to an unbeliever? Is there an unbeliever listening to me? You are yet in these detestable things! This is your life! To escape from it, my friend, there is only one way: look to Christ! His blood must wash you from your sins! His righteousness must clothe you! Come to Christ! 'Lord give me this righteousness! Lord wash my sins away in your blood. Forgive me my sins, receive me now, take me to the Father, make me accepted in yourself!' *And he will!* And then you, too, will be in the same position as the rest of the people I've addressed in this small talk.

We are believers! Now let us look to Jesus! Let us arm ourselves with this attitude! Let us think upon Christ dying for us, and us dying in him! And the more we think upon him, and look to him, the less attractive will the world become, and the more we shall live to the glory of his name! Indeed, as he goes on to say, Peter, in verse 11: 'All things' – 'in all things, God maybe praised through Jesus Christ. To him be the glory and the power for ever and ever. Amen'.

Start by thinking upon Christ, looking to Christ – not trying; not looking to law, but looking to Christ! – and you will end up living to the praise of Jesus Christ: To [him be] the glory and power – in praise of God for ever and ever. Amen!

# Antinomianism: What Will Stop It?

*The grace of God that brings salvation has appeared to all men. It teaches us to say 'No' to ungodliness and worldly passions, and to live self-controlled, upright and godly lives in this present age, while we wait for the blessed hope – the glorious appearing of our great God and Saviour, Jesus Christ, who gave himself for us to redeem us from all wickedness and to purify for himself a people that are his very own, eager to do what is good (Tit. 2:11-14).*

I wish to speak to you for a few minutes on Titus chapter 2 and verse 12; Titus chapter 2 and verse 12. Paul writes to Titus and says this – well, go back – from verse 11: 'For the grace of God that brings salvation has appeared to all men. It teaches us to say "No" to ungodliness and worldly passions, and to live self-controlled, upright and godly lives in this present age, while we wait for the blessed hope'; and so on.

It is these words I want to concentrate on, though: 'It teaches us to say "No" to ungodliness and worldly passions, and to live self-controlled, upright and godly lives in this present age'.

'Us', 'us'. The apostle is speaking about himself and Titus, and, of course, in this connection, he's writing to Titus to encourage him, to instruct him, to nerve him, and to stir him, for his ministry and his work – the commission he has given him to carry out leaving him in Crete. For Paul is saying here [that] we need to see the believers at Crete – believers everywhere – we need to see believers saying 'No' to ungodliness and worldly passions, and we need to see these believers living positive lives to the glory of God, practical in godliness and spirituality.

And, of course, it's not just in the apostle's day. It's true for us today! I, as a believer – you, if you're a believer, listening to me – one who trusts the Lord Jesus Christ; you have a living faith in him, you've passed from death to life, you are justified, you're your right with God through faith in the Lord Jesus Christ.

Well, then, we have now to live as new creatures: 'If any man is in Christ Jesus he is a new creation. Behold, old things are

passed away. Behold, all things are become new!' We live a life
to the glory of God. Now what will teach us? What will instruct
us? What will nerve us? What will stir us? What will move us?
What will motivate us to this godly life? The negative: to say
'No' to ungodliness, worldliness, pagan-living, hedonism, living
for self, pleasure, living for lusts. And positively: to live
controlled, upright, godly, spiritual lives in this present age, this
ungodly age, this worldly age in which we live, this Satanic-
dominated, Satan-dominated age, the blindness, the ignorance,
the darkness all around us? How can we live as lights shining in
this present evil age, waiting for the Lord Jesus Christ to come
again – saying 'No' to what world offers us, and saying 'Yes' to
all God demands of us in his word?

What will move us to it? What does Paul say to Titus? What
does he say he wants him to preach – as he says in verse 15:
'These, then, are the things you should teach. Encourage and
rebuke with all authority. Do not let anyone despise you'.
'Titus: this is what I want you to preach! This is what I want to
understand, first of all! This is what I want to know for yourself,
first of all! First and foremost, before you ever try to teach
anybody else, learn it for yourself! What will enable you to
stand out from this present evil age and live for the glory of
God?'

Well, this is a vital question. We know that for all who are right
with God – justified by faith in the Lord Jesus Christ – God has
created good works for us to live and do in this present evil age.
We have to live to the glory of God. We can't be antinomians.
We can't be lawless, and libertines, and live like the world.
What's going to teach us to say 'No' to the world, and say 'Yes'
to God? In short: What is going to make me a sanctified man?

Well, here, as I've said on many occasions, there are two
systems, if you like, two ways, that are offered to believers. The
common, the usual, way is that – and the way that seems by
human logic to make sense – is to teach the believers that they
are under the law of God, the ten commandments, in particular,
the moral law. Live as those who are under this law! Bear in
mind the blessings that come from this law; bear in mind the

curses that come, the punishments that come, from disobeying this law. Rules, regulations, often although it is said 'the ten commandments', often other rules and regulations, man-made rules and regulations, are imposed upon believers. But it's by rule and rote, and ceremony of obedience – conformity, rather – that kind of thing – that we shall produce this kind of saying 'No' to ungodliness, and 'Yes' to God. Fear is at the bottom of this motive. That's one way. If you think I've made all that up, then you'd better read John Calvin,[1] and see how he called the law a whip to smite us as lazy asses to drive us to godliness. And you'd better listen to modern preaching, where so often it's: 'Do these things! Don't do those things! Do the others!' And it's commandment, commandment and commandment; recipe, recipe, recipe!

But I ask you: What does *Paul* say here? What will teach me to say 'No'? Is it the law? What will teach me to say 'Yes' to God? Is it the law? 'It is', says Paul (verse 11), 'the grace of God that brings salvation that will teach me (verse 11 and 12) to say "No" to ungodliness, and say "Yes" to God'. Do you hear that? The grace of God – the grace of God – will teach me to say 'No' to sin, and 'Yes' to holiness. The grace of God will teach me to say 'No' to the world, and ' Yes' to God. The grace of God will teach me to say 'No' to what the world's pundits teach, and to say 'Yes' to what the Spirit says in his word.

The grace of God! This is what Titus has to preach. Preach the grace of God! 'The grace of God' – it's often said is the undeserved kindness of God to us. I don't think it is. I think it's more than that! I think it's the kindness of God to me when I deserve the exact opposite of kindness. For, I read in Ephesians 2, that by nature I'm a child of wrath, under the wrath of God, and yet in his love and his mercy, as Paul goes on, in Ephesians 2, to say: 'But God, who is rich in love, for his great love wherewith he loved us. For by grace are you saved through faith, and that not of yourselves: it is the gift of God'.

---

[1] See the first chapter of this present work.

'Stress this', Paul says to Titus. Let this sink into you mind! Make sure you make this the principal thing of your preaching: Christ, the grace of God in Christ, the mercy of God in Christ, 'the glorious appearing of our great God and Saviour, Jesus Christ, who gave himself for us to redeem us from all wickedness and to purify for himself a people that are his very own, eager to do what is good'. Stress these things! Preach these things! Lift up Christ in his sacrifice, in his death, in his blood being shed, in his burial, in his resurrection, his intercession, and his coming again. Preach Christ! Stress the grace of God! And as the believers hear this, and meditate upon it, and feel it, they shall be enabled to say 'No' to the world, and 'Yes' to God.

Believer! Are you tempted to sin? Of course you are! Then listen! Hear the grace of God! Look to Christ in the grace of God! Think about the mercy that God has showered upon you, and shown to you in Christ!

Believer! Do you have doubts? Of course you do! Then look to the grace of God! Look to Christ! 'Look full in his wonderful face!' Is the world attractive to you? 'Look full in his wonderful face, and the things of earth will grow strangely dim in the light of his glory and grace'.

Do you lack assurance, believer? Are you low and cast down and depressed? Are you backsliding? Do you want your heart warmed? Then look to Christ! Dwell upon his grace! Think on him and his mercy to you. And let your heart be melted again, as Christ, in his grace, giving himself for your salvation, [and] it [the thought of all this] comes into your heart and into your mind, sinks into your soul, and works itself out in your life.

Do you want to be holy? Then think upon Christ and his grace!

Do I address any preachers? Are you a legal preacher, my friend? Are you preaching rules and regulations and laws? There are commandments in the gospel, it is true. There's commandments all over the New Testament, yes, but coupled with all those commandments you will find this: the mercy of God, the grace of God. This is the motive – always – for sanctification. Give up preaching law *per se*. Preach the gospel, my brother. Preach Christ! This will sanctify, edify, confirm, protect, build up the saints.

Is there any unbeliever listening to me? Will you listen to me, my friend? Give up trying to earn your salvation! There is no salvation in 'doing'! There's no salvation in effort and trying! Look to Christ! Trust the grace of God in Christ! It sanctifies the saints, but it will also, in the beginning, save the sinner: 'For by grace are you saved through faith'. Look to Christ, then! Trust him! Turn from your sin, crying out for mercy! Then you, too, will become a child of God, a saint – and, having become a child of God, you will join us then.

And whether we're preaching or hearing – whatever it is – as believers, we shall be continuing to lift up Christ to others – and to ourselves, first of all – looking unto Jesus: trusting, looking, waiting upon, meditating upon, the grace of God in Christ. For the grace of God will teach us to say 'No' to the world, and 'Yes' to God.

# Antinomianism: The Ultimate Cure

*Since, then, you have been raised with Christ, set your hearts on things above, where Christ is seated at the right hand of God. Set your minds on things above, not on earthly things. For you died, and your life is now hidden with Christ in God. When Christ, who is your life, appears, then you also will appear with him in glory. Put to death, therefore, whatever belongs to your flesh: sexual immorality, impurity, lust, evil desires and greed, which is idolatry. Because of these, the wrath of God is coming. You used to walk in these ways, in the life you once lived. But now you must rid yourselves of all such things as these: anger, rage, malice, slander, and filthy language from your lips. Do not lie to each other, since you have taken off your old self with its practices and have put on the new self, which is being renewed in knowledge in the image of its creator. Here there is no Greek or Jew, circumcised or uncircumcised, barbarian, Scythian, slave or free, but Christ is all, and is in all. Therefore, as God's chosen people, holy and dearly loved, clothe yourselves with compassion, kindness, humility, gentleness and patience. Bear with each other and forgive whatever grievances you may have against one another. Forgive as the Lord forgave you. And over all these virtues put on love, which binds them all together in perfect unity. Let the peace of Christ rule in your hearts, since as members of one body you were called to peace. And be thankful. Let the word of Christ dwell in you richly as you teach and admonish one another with all wisdom, and as you sing psalms, hymns and spiritual songs with gratitude in your hearts to God. And whatever you do, whether in word or deed, do it all in the name of the Lord Jesus, giving thanks to God the Father through him (Col. 3:1-17)*

I'd like a few minutes with you, if I may, speaking on Colossians chapter 3, and verses 1 to 17. Colossians 3:1-17.

I have called this small address: 'Antinomianism: The Ultimate Cure'. 'Antinomianism: The Ultimate Cure'.

Some of you may have been wondering, as you've heard this word 'antinomianism', you may have wondered what it really is. What is this 'antinomianism'? How does it show itself?

Well, I think the apostle, here – Paul – gives us, in a few words, a very full, clear, description of the kind of lifestyle, the kind of habit, the kind of attitude, the kind of mindset, the kind of way of living, that you can find in an antinomian. I'm thinking of verse 5. Now, the apostle here is telling believers what they must *not* do; what must *not* be in their life. But, the things he's describing here are in fact the things that belong to this thing called 'antinomianism'. 'Whatever belongs to your members on earth: sexual immorality, impurity, lust, evil desires and greed, which is idolatry'.

Have look at that for a moment. I say to you that describes the kind of behaviour, the kind of lifestyle you would find in an antinomian man, or an antinomian woman: living for this life, living for earthly pleasures, living as the worldly man, the worldly woman, lives; living for sexual immorality, indulgence of every kind, lusting, greed; and so on, and so on. I think you can see here very clearly the kind of lifestyle, the kind of approach to life that the antinomian will reveal: he is, she is, carnal – acting as an unbeliever, acting as a pagan.

Now I know some misapply that text in Corinthians about... when.. Paul writes to the Corinthians there: 'You are carnal, and so on', and they think that Paul is giving the description of a perfectly acceptable kind of Christian life. If you are one such of an opinion, my friend, you're completely mistaken! Paul is not describing that which is acceptable! As here, he is describing something which is abominable! You want to know my opinion about this kind of lifestyle, in a professing believer? It comes from hell! It's Satanic! It's diabolical! It's utterly wrong! It's sinful! It's wicked! It's evil! Have I been clear enough?

This kind of lifestyle is not only *disappointing* in a believer: it is utterly unacceptable! In fact, if a man or a woman lives like this, they may profess all they will about being Christian, about being a believer, but their life contradicts their profession. 'If any man is in Christ, he is a new creation. Old things are passed away. Behold, all things are become new!' Paul says, in verse 7: 'You used to walk in these ways, in the life you once lived'. This is how you once lived. You were pagans! But now you're converted, you *do* not live like this! You *cannot* live like this! You *must* not live like this!

I hope I've made myself clear!

What does Paul want? He wants the very opposite of these things. He wants us to cultivate the very opposite of these things. And he gives us many do's and many do-not's. There are commands in the gospel. Believers are commanded. The Bible is full of these commands. The New Testament is full of these commands to believers.

But this is not the point I am after here. I think we're all agreed at this point – well, I hope we are, anyway! If you are a believer, then my friend, you recognise that you must live a life that conforms to Christ, and not to the world. You must live a life in obedience to God's word, not a life that conforms to the standards of this present age. I'm sure – well, I hope, anyway – I can take it for granted, that that is a given among us.

The great issue is this, the great question... is: How can I reach this standard? How can I attain to this? What will motivate me to it? What will move me to it? What will give me energy and power to do it? What is the way that will enable me to reach this glorious position where I don't live like pagans [do], I live like believers do – I don't live like the world; I live like Christ?

You see, it goes deeper than what I've said. If you look at verse 8, you will find that Paul goes down deeper and more inward: anger, rage, malice, slander, filthy language, lying; and all this kind of thing. How can I reach this standard – where I don't live like this, I don't think like this, I don't act like this, I don't speak like this, I don't spend my time like this?

This where the Christian world divides sharply into two. The majority of evangelical and Reformed believers, following the teaching of John Calvin – whether they know it or whether they don't – think that the best way, the right way, to produce this spirituality is to give believers the law of Moses – particularly the ten commandments, which they call 'the moral law'. Now some teachers are overt about this, and most definite in their writings and in their teachings. The Confessions say it – and I mean by that the Westminster Confession, the 1689 Baptist Confession (Particular Baptist Confession) – these sorts of Confessions. And these teachers, the great systematic theology's, the great teachers in the churches, are, by and large, are men of the law.

Calvin – who, as I say, was the principal architect of this system, whether men know it or not – likened the law to a whip; and we, as believers, he likened to lazy mules, lazy donkeys, lazy asses – and as a lazy ass won't move unless you clout him a whip, so the believer needs to be whipped with the law. I'm using Calvin's picture. If you don't believe me, read his writings! If you want to read extracts from his works, you can see my own book *Christ Is All*, where you will see it fully set out and documented. This is what he said. And many of his followers have said very similar things: We must hold the law before our eyes! We must preach the law, teach the law! And that will make us a sanctified, godly people![1] As I say, some are overtly like this; but many – the vast majority of – teachers are much more incipient, much more subdued. It's there – at a lower level – but it's there all the same.

I want to be useful. I want to be as clear as I can, and helpful as I can to you. Let me describe a sermon that I've heard recently. It was a sermon about 40 minutes long, and it was based – and it came from – the book of Daniel. And I think I'm – well, I know I am – I'm distilling fairly what this man said. He wanted us to be a spiritual people. I'm sure of that! And this is what he said: We must read our Bible regularly, and we must say our prayers regularly. He used the words 'quiet time'. We must 'ring fence our quiet time'. We must be regular in our prayers, and regular in our Scripture reading. Three times a day should we pray. And for 40 minutes – well, for 38 minutes, I should say – of this discourse, *that* was what he was stressing, and labouring, and making clear to us: You keep up your Bible reading, you keep

---

[1] In this present volume, see the first chapter for several extracts from Calvin and others.

up your prayers. And the implication is, that, as you keep up your Bible reading, and keep up your prayers, you will grow in grace and the knowledge of Christ.

I don't know what planet that man's living on! Let me say at once: I have nothing to say against Bible reading, nothing to say against saying prayers! Do I need to say that? I have everything to say *for* Bible reading, and everything to say *for* saying my prayers! I have nothing to say against ring-fencing times when we might give ourselves to God! Nothing must interrupt us in our coming to God, and worship, and hearing from him in his word, and saying prayers, and praying to him! I don't know if I am making myself clear. I'm going to be misunderstood, I'm sure! People will think I'm speaking against saying prayers and reading the Bible! Not at all!

But I will say this, my friend: 'You can keep your 'quiet time' as regular as clockwork – *but it won't make you, in itself, it won't make you a spiritual man*! The truth is, you can be on your knees – and have impure thoughts! You can be reading your Bible – and your mind be full of worldliness! You can be in a pulpit doing it! You can be doing any of these exercises, carrying out any of these exercises, in a very strict and a very disciplined way, and yet you can still be guilty of these things: impurity, lust, evil desires, rage, anger, malice, slander, filthy language – and all that kind of stuff – in your heart and mind!

I'm saying to you: You can preach conformity to people, make them obey rules and keep to regulations, and it may look as though they're spiritual. *But it doesn't necessarily follow that they are!* They may be wearing the right colour suit, they may be carrying the right version of the Bible, the right hymnbook, they may be regular in attendance, but it does not necessarily follow that you are a spiritual person.

I know of a person who went to her pastor – I'm not saying that she should do this – but she went to her pastor, and she thought, she said, she was backsliding. And the pastor said: 'Well, you can't be', he said, 'because you're coming to the meetings'! You see what was in his mind: Because you are attending meetings, that makes you spiritual. I don't know what planet that man was living on! You can be completely carnal, sitting in a pew, with a Bible opened. You can be carnal in a pulpit, preaching!

Conformity to rules will not make me spiritual. But I put it to you that the majority of teachers in the Christian world teach, in one form or another, sanctification, godliness, by rules and regulation, the law of God!

I'm not saying a word against the law of God. It's part of Scripture! I'm not saying a word against Bible reading, or prayers, or chapel attendance, or hearing the gospel. I'm not saying a word... I'm say a lot for it, all for it! And there are commandments here! But what does Paul tell me here is the motive, and the great stirrer, and the great energizer, and the great means, whereby I shall attain to this standard?

Well I only have to read it to you. I have only a short time, and therefore I'll just read it to you. But let me read it to you – verse 1:

Since, then, you have been raised with the Christ, set your hearts on things above, where Christ is seated at the right hand of God. Set your mind on things above, not on earthly things. For you died, and your life is now hidden with Christ in God. When Christ, who is your life appears, then you also will appear with him in glory.

Can you see the difference, my friend?

Make sure you say your regular prayers! Make sure you read your Bible! I'm not saying a word against it – but is *that* going to make me holy?

Set your mind upon Christ! Set your heart upon Christ – his coming again for you! He died for you! He loves you with an everlasting love! He prays for you now! He's interceding for you! Think upon Christ! Think upon Christ! Think upon the glory to come!

Or how about verse 12: 'As God's chosen people' – think of your election – 'holy and dearly loved' – God has loved you with an everlasting love! He has separated you from the world!

– 'clothe yourselves with compassion' – and all the rest of it – 'kindness, humility, bear with each other'! Why? 'Forgive each other'! Why? 'Forgive as the Lord forgave you'! 'Let the peace of Christ rule in your hearts! Let the word of Christ dwelling in you richly as you teach one another, admonish one another, with all wisdom' – and so on – 'singing psalms and hymns and spiritual songs with gratitude in your hearts to God. And whatever you do, whether in word or deed, do it all in the name of the Lord Jesus, giving thanks to God the Father through him'!

Once again, I don't know whether I'm making myself clear to you! But to me, there's a world of difference between conforming to regular patterns of quiet times, keeping rules and regulations, and setting my mind upon Christ, my heart upon him, thinking what he's done for me, what he's doing for me now, what he will do for me – in the years to come, what he will do for me in eternity – what he has done in me – thinking upon Christ! Is there anything here about rules and regulations?

Well, there is! In verse 20, in the previous chapter! Let me read it to you:

Since you died with Christ to the basic principles of this world, why, as though you still belonged to it, do you submit to its rules: Do not handle! Do not taste! Do not touch! these are all destined to perish with use, because they are based on human commands and teachings.

If you may say: 'Well, the ten commandments are not human commands and regulations and teachings', I quite agree! But the same principle will apply: you can have all the codes you like even the highest and the best, the noblest, code – 'such regulations indeed have an appearance of wisdom, with their self-imposed worship, their false humility and their harsh treatment of the body, but they lack any value in restraining sensual indulgence'. You've only got to look at the Jewish nation. They had the law – *but did it make them a godly people?* The law? Did it make them godly? It did not!

Rules and regulations will not make me conform to Christ. It's got to come from within, working out – not from without, trying to work in.

And this is 'the ultimate', I say. Why? Because I [deliberately] missed out the *great* text! And it is the central text! And its verse 11: 'Christ'! (chapter 3, Colossians 3, and verse 11): 'Christ is all, and is in all'.

I hope I've made it clear: the difference between one method – rule, regulation, conform! Christ! Christ is! Christ is all, and in all! Look to Christ! 'Looking unto Jesus, the author and the finisher of our faith'. 'Consider him!' 'Set your minds and your hearts upon him!' 'Look full into his wonderful face, and the things of earth will grow strangely dim, in the light of his glory and grace'.

How can I do this, and sin against the Lord! It is Christ, I'm sinning against! How can I offend God who loved me so much! I am the temple of the Holy Spirit! God the Spirit's in me: How can I do these things! How can I say these things! I can't go to these places! Why not? Because I'm a Christian! I'm in Christ, and Christ is in me! And I'm looking to Jesus, the author and the finisher of my faith! He is all!

I'm addressing you now, my friend, and you are either a believer or an believer.

If you are a believer, you must not conform to this world, you have this command. How should you turn away from this world, and be conformed to Christ? Looking to Christ, trusting Christ! Yes, read your Bible; of course, you must! Say your prayers, yes. But don't you realise that even in all these rules and regulations, what you must do above all is set your mind and your heart and your affections upon the Lord Jesus! Think of him! Speak of him! Sing of him! Dwell upon him! And you will grow like him! And one day, you will be transformed completely, in glory, to be with him forever, and like him forever.

Unbeliever: we once, too, all of us who are believers, were once just like you – far off from God. How can you be saved from your sins? If you go to Islam, that will not save you! If you go to Buddhism, that won't save you! If you go to baptism, the Lord's table, church attendance, Bible reading, prayers – all those sorts of things – you can do what you will, my friend: it won't save you! You must look unto Jesus! You must trust him!

So, it's the same word – it's the *ultimate* for us all. If I'm a sinner, to be saved, I must look to Jesus, and I shall be saved. So, is there an unbeliever listening to me? Look to Jesus, now, and he will save you.

And then I say, finally, to all believers: 'Since then you have been raised with Christ, set your hearts on things above'! Set your hearts upon Christ! 'Christ is all, and in all'! And as you look to him, and dwell upon him, you will be more and more conformed to him.

And all will be as it says in verse 17: 'Whatever you do, whether in word or deed, do it all in the name of the Lord Jesus, giving thanks to God the Father through him'.

# Reviews

# Christ Is All: No Sanctification By The Law

John Calvin inherited the doctrines of the medieval Roman Church. In particular, he inherited that Church's view of the law of God, given to Israel through Moses on Sinai. Calvin took the Church's teaching on this, as it had been developed by Thomas Aquinas, and tweaked it to produce a Reformed threefold-use of the law in the new covenant. Some Anabaptists and others resisted him at the time, but they were heavily out-gunned, and Calvin's system has dominated the Reformed and evangelical world ever since. Millions, who have never read a word of Calvin, many of whom would shudder at the very mention of his name, nevertheless, are, on the law, Calvinists – even though they may not know it.

David Gay contends that Calvin was wrong on the law, and this has had serious consequences. Gay is concerned, in particular, with the Reformer's third use of the law – which is, said Calvin, to sanctify the believer. Gay disagrees. In this book, he probes Calvin's system, exposes it to the light of Scripture, and shows where it departs from the New Testament. He also demonstrates the utter inadequacy of the escape routes used by the Reformed to get round awkward passages of Scripture.

Turning from the negative, Gay then looks at every major New Testament passage dealing with the believer and the law. Next, he sets out scriptural teaching on the true way of sanctification for the believer. This, he shows, is not by the law of Moses; rather, it is by the law of Christ in the hands of the Holy Spirit. Indeed, as Gay makes clear, the law of Christ is, ultimately, Christ himself. Hence his chosen title: 'Christ Is All'. Having set out the believer's rule, he then answers seven objections levelled against it.

Gay does not pretend that this book is an easy read. But he hopes it will prove a profitable read. And even if others do not agree with him on every point, until they have read what he has to say, it can hardly be fair, can it, to dismiss him out of hand as an antinomian?

## Some reviews

5.0 out of 5 stars. **Deals thoroughly with Christian sanctification in Christ rather than Moses (Law)**, 16 Aug 2013. By Terence Clarke: *David Gay thoroughly deals with the biblical concept and application of sanctification (imparted righteousness) which he reveals is in Christ alone. He demolishes the teaching of the reformers and those that follow on this issue that sanctification is by the 10 Commandments. He shows that just as in justification Christ is all and as far as the sanctification of believers is concerned 'Christ is in all'. This is anything but an antinomian approach but emphasises the power of Christ in the Christian's life. David's style is unusual in that it displays a preacher's approach to delivery but is fresh and direct. He does repeat his arguments throughout the book so that the reader should be in no doubt of them or misunderstand them. He introduces briefly his amillennialist view on Israel which, I find, is not argued with the same biblical thoroughness as the main subject. Recommended for all those who have a true interest in biblical sanctification and the whole work of Christ.*

5.0 out of 5 stars. **Demolishes Reformed view of sanctification by law**, November 12, 2013. By Dan Trotter: *Best and most thorough book on New Covenant Theology I have ever seen. Completely demolishes the erroneous Reformed doctrine of sanctification by law.*

4.0 out of 5 stars. **At last a view of "New Covenant" Sanctification**, August 30, 2013. By Moe Bergeron: *"Antinomian!" is a hideous charge that is levelled at those who do not believe in any use of Sinai's Law for the saint's sanctification. The fact of the matter is that anyone who subscribes to such a use, including a third use, of Sinai's Law denies the clear biblical teaching of Romans 7:6 and 2 Corinthians 3. The written code and the way of the Spirit are opposed to one another. In the apostle Peter's 2nd letter and in the 1st chapter he explains New Covenant sanctification. Learn of Christ! David Gay's work is a must read for all who understand that the Lutheran/Reformed debate is not Law vs. Gospel. It truly is Letter vs. Spirit.*

5.0 out of 5 stars. **Life changing!**, July 20, 2013. By Dr. John S. Waldrip (Monrovia, CA United States): *David H. J. Gay writes in a way most can easily follow to show that an error concerning the Mosaic Law has found its way through Thomas Aquinas and John Calvin into mainstream Protestant thought. Gay shows the error of this and points the reader ever and always to the Lord Jesus Christ as the Object the divine Means by which the believer's sanctification is accomplished. I would give this book six stars if the author had left out the final chapter of the book.*

5.0 out of 5 stars. **Insightful, courageous and clear**, 27 Aug 2013. By Mr. Rod Angus: *The Reformed teaching that the OT law, especially the 10 Commandments, is the Christian's standard and perfect rule for obedience, when not overtly taught, is nevertheless the insipient ingredient lurking in the minds of many believers. The belief that the Law is an aid to sanctification is a lie. The law dis-empowers and condemns, but never sanctifies. David Gay has written a unique book exposing this Reformed spell that has been cast over the Church. As he writes 'The same grace that saves..also sanctifies' Grace wins the love of the heart in a way that the law never could. 'The Law of Christ' is 'a real law. Love is its goal, love is its motive'. My only real problem with David's wonderful book is his continued allegiance to the Augustine-Calvin Christologically deficient teaching on election. I have already contacted him over this, to which he graciously replied. I hope he sniffs this one out in the same way as he has exposed the lie concerning the believer and the law. Nevertheless, this is an outstanding piece of writing. Thank you David.*

# Four 'Antinomians' Tried And Vindicated

'THIS BOOK IS DANGEROUS! EATON, DELL, CRISP AND SALTMARSH WERE ANTINOMIANS. THEIR WORKS SHOULD NEVER HAVE SEEN THE LIGHT OF DAY, AND SHOULD NOT BE RE-PUBLISHED NOW!'

So it will be said. David Gay disagrees. Strongly! Judging by these works, which he has distilled and annotated, they preached the gospel of our Lord Jesus Christ in all its fullness, and with power. What they said in these sermons makes vital reading for all Christians!

These men were not perfect, of course, but they glorified Christ, they got to the heart of justification by faith, they set out the wonder of the new covenant, they preached to help believers find assurance, and they showed the need for, and the way of, sanctification - which is not by the law, but by the gospel. For all this, they ought to be commended, not blackballed!

ARE YOU WILLING TO TAKE THE RISK, READ THIS BOOK AND JUDGE FOR YOURSELF? IT MIGHT WELL CHANGE YOUR LIFE FOR GOOD, AND IN MORE WAYS THAN ONE! WILL YOU OPEN YOUR MIND, HEART AND LIFE TO THE LORD JESUS CHRIST AND HIS GLORIOUS, LIBERATING GOSPEL?

## A review

5.0 out of 5 stars. By Jonathan H. Zens: *I had the privilege of meeting David Gay in August, 2013, at the 14th Searching Together Conference in Elgin IL. His sessions on 2 Cor 3 & 4 were uplifting! I have perused several of David's previous books – "The Priesthood of All Believers: Slogan or Substance", "The Pastor – Does He Exist?" and "Christ Is All: No Sanctification by the Law" – with great profit. "Four Antinomians", though an historical study, nevertheless affords the opportunity to focus on some very important issues – has Christ actually removed forever all condemnation for those in Christ? must sinners be "prepared" for the gospel by Law-preaching? Of the "Four," I'm most familiar with Tobias Crisp. After I wrote what many called "ground-breaking" articles in 1977-1978 ("Is There A 'Covenant of Grace?" and "Crucial Thoughts on Law in the New Covenant"), several well-known Reformed Baptists (Walt Chantry and Al Martin) called me an "antinomian." In 1978, Walt Chantry wrote me a long letter and designated me as "neo-dispensational" and "neo-antinomian." I spent hours in the Vanderbilt Divinity Library in Nashville researching antinomianism in history, focusing on Tobias Crisp. I concluded then, as David Gay has now, that calling Crisp "antinomian" was a false accusation. I sent a detailed reply to Walt which suggested that the appellation of "antinomian" was inappropriate for Crisp and myself. David Gay has done us a tremendous service by documenting the freeness of grace in Christ as proclaimed by these four often maligned men. What I especially appreciate about David's presentation is his even-handedness. He clearly unfolds where he agrees with these four, where he disagrees with them, and where he believes them to have been unwise in the way they expressed certain sentiments. I highly recommend this book. It sheds light on vital issues that have come to the top cyclically in church history.*

Made in the USA
Lexington, KY
10 September 2017